Dessert

EXPRESS

100 SWEET TREATS YOU CAN MAKE IN 30 MINUTES OR LESS

LAUREN CHATTMAN

PHOTOGRAPHS BY ALEXANDRA GRABLEWSKI

 **The Taunton Press**
Inspiration for hands-on living®

The Taunton Press, Inc.,
63 South Main Street, PO Box 5506,
Newtown, CT 06470-5506
e-mail: tp@taunton.com

Editor: Pamela Hoenig
Jacket/Cover design: L49 Design
Interior design: L49 Design
Layout: Kimberly Shake
Photographer: Alexandra Grablewski
Copy editor: Li Agen
Indexer: Heidi Blough

Library of Congress Cataloging-in-Publication Data
Chattman, Lauren.
  Dessert express : 100 sweet treats you can make in 30 minutes or less /
Lauren Chattman.
      p. cm.
  Includes bibliographical references and index.
  ISBN 978-1-60085-018-9 (alk. paper)

  1. Desserts. 2. Quick and easy cookery. I. Title.

TX773.C47155 2008
641.8'6--dc22

                        2007048860

Printed in China
10 9 8 7 6 5 4 3 2 1

The following manufacturers/names appearing in *Dessert Express* are trademarks: Almond Joy®, Amaretti®, Andes®,
Ben & Jerry's®, Boylan's®, Bundt®, Butterfinger's®, Carr's®, Chips Ahoy®, Ciao Bella®, Coco Lopez®, Cracker Jack®,
Easy-Bake® oven, Goya®, Grand Marnier®, Häagen Dazs®, Heath Bar®, Jules Destrooper®, Kahlúa®, King Arthur®,
Kraft® caramels, Mallomars®, Marshmallow Fluff®, Nabisco®, Newman's Own®, Nilla® wafers, Nutella®, Planter's®,
Raisinets®, Red Hots®, Reese's® Peanut Butter Cups®, Reese's Pieces®, Skor®, Walkers®

Acknowledgments

To Pam Hoenig, thanks for everything. I've benefited so
much from your wisdom and experience over the years! As
always, agent Angela Miller provided her special brand of
support before, during, and after the writing of this book.
Thanks to the great team at The Taunton Press—Li Agen,
Katie Benoit, Nora Fuentes, Audrey Locorotondo, Erica
Sanders-Foege, Amy Griffin, Alison Wilkes, Sharon Zagata—
for making everything so easy. Alexandra Grablewski's photos
perfectly captured the appeal of these quick desserts. Thanks
to assistant Todd Bonne, stylist Leslie Seigel and food stylist
Brian Preston-Campbell for their help at the shoot.
And thanks, finally, to Jack, Rose, and Eve for their
great ideas and courage in trying anything sweet in the
service of this project.

Contents

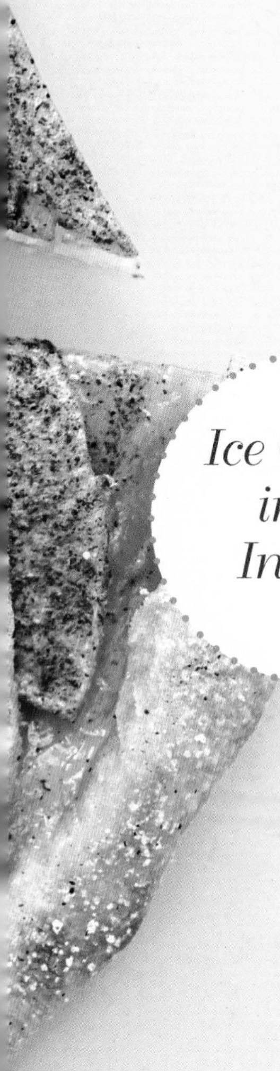

THE FAST TRACK

Dessert

A few years ago, when my older daughter was about eight years old, she invited a friend over for an after-school play date.

It was going so well she asked if the friend could stay for dinner. I was just making a pot of rice and beans, I told the friend, but she was welcome to join us if her mom said it was okay. The little girl called her mother, who I knew only by her reputation as a great cook and hostess, and said excitedly, "Mom, Lauren invited us to dinner! Can we come?" The mother immediately accepted this spur-of-the-moment invitation, and said she'd be over in 45 minutes. Eek! I hurried to get my rice and beans cooking and wondered what else I could offer that would make it seem as if I had really meant to invite a grown-up to my house.

Nothing could be done about the humble main course, but maybe I could pull a dessert out of my hat that would make my guest feel special. What about a couple of bananas? I had no other fresh fruit in the house. Rummaging through the pantry, I grabbed a can of cream of coconut, whisked in some cocoa powder, and warmed the mixture on top of the stove. *Voilà!* Chocolate-Coconut Fondue with sliced bananas. The tropical flavors would even complement my Caribbean rice and beans. Done with dessert in less than 15 minutes, I still had time to set the table and pour myself a drink. The night was a success: My new friend was grateful for the nourishing dinner and was truly amazed by its fun and unexpected ending.

My mom used to cook from a column in *The New York Times* called "The 60-Minute Gourmet." Today that time frame seems quaint. Now the majority of cooks have less than an hour to spend in the kitchen, sometimes much less. And dessert, a luxury rather than a necessity, is the first thing to get squeezed out. When I was up against the wall with my uninvited but very welcome guest, I could have skipped dessert entirely. But no matter how rushed I am, I always want something sweet at the end of the meal, to complete my pleasure and show hospitality. After I had some success with express desserts like my Chocolate-Coconut Fondue, I challenged myself to make 99 more desserts that were similarly quick, so I would never be at a loss for something sweet. This book is the result, a collection of recipes, each one of which can be on the table in 30 minutes or less.

The recipes range from after-school snacks to dinner party showstoppers, because I like to be prepared for every occasion. With each one, I carefully considered how to get the most impact with the least amount of work. I didn't want them to be boring! Sometimes a little salt or pepper did the trick. So a homey butterscotch pudding gets a sprinkling of sea salt to enhance its caramel flavor, and Molten Chocolate-Chili Cakes have a dash of cayenne pepper to spark them up. Occasionally, I'd use a trick learned from a professional pastry chef to invigorate an old idea. The shards of sweet and crunchy phyllo dough for the Deconstructed Apricot & Ricotta Tarts were inspired by a phyllo dough garnish I learned from former White House pastry chef Roland Mesnier, who has taught me so much over the years. When I could, I'd use ingredients from around the world to create a simple dessert with intriguing flavors. Sliced mango bathed in coconut milk and honey is as simple a dessert as you can make, but also surprising and unusual to most people. I hope you'll agree that with desserts like this in the half-hour range there's no reason to skip the trip.

☀ EXPRESS ROUTES TO QUICK DESSERTS ☀

As I developed the recipes for this book, I realized I was consistently relying on a few shortcuts to arrive at a wide variety of desserts in 30 minutes. Here are some of my favorite express routes to satisfying anybody's sweet tooth. You can see how they work in my recipes, and you may want to try them to speed up some of your own recipes:

Downsize

It takes less time to make sixteen Green Tea & White Chocolate Truffles than it does to make sixty. Likewise, making twelve Fig Shortbread Bites is quicker than making three dozen. Anytime that it made sense to cut the yield of a recipe to make it more manageable, I did so, often with significant time savings.

Not only did I shrink yields, I often miniaturized the desserts themselves. A full-size Bundt® cake can take an hour and 15 minutes to bake. Divide the batter into six small portions to make mini Bundt cakes and you can have them in and out of the oven in 20 minutes.

Turn Up the Heat

It stands to reason that cakes and cookies will bake more quickly at higher temperatures. So I gravitated toward baked goods that would do well in hotter ovens. Thus, an Apple Pizza made with sturdy frozen pizza dough bakes at 500 degrees for 15 minutes, as do Fruit Shortcakes, which take a mere 12 minutes. I did sometimes miscalculate, burning a batch of Cocoa Madeleines in a 425-degree oven before baking them to perfection at 375 degrees, and winding up with "blackbottom" rather than Blueberry Upside-Down Cakes after baking my first batch at 450 degrees. But in hopes of shaving minutes off of baking time whenever possible, I continued to push the envelope with items that usually bake at a relatively low temperature, nudging the thermostat to 375 degrees for Mini Goat Cheese Cakes when most cheesecakes bake at 325 degrees or lower.

Chill Out

Often, I'd prepare a dessert in well under 30 minutes, only to find myself waiting impatiently for it to cool down to a comfortable temperature for eating. So I did the same thing I do when I want to chill a bottle of white wine in minutes: I got out a big bowl, filled it with ice and water, and submerged the bottom of the hot pan in an ice bath to quickly bring down the dessert's temperature. Everything from Mini Goat Cheese Cakes to tapioca pudding to Greek Honey & Sesame Candy got this treatment when the clock was ticking.

Sometimes, using the freezer made more sense. Small items like Chocolate-Covered Grapes and Almond Joy® Bonbons needed just 5 to 10 minutes of chilling before they were ready to serve.

Think Outside the Box—or the Oven

If it was impossible to bake a batch of cookies in the oven in under 30 minutes, I'd try to bake them somewhere else. A waffle iron can cook cookie dough in a minute and a half. Drop dough into hot oil and you can have cloudlike deep-fried ricotta fritters in about 3 minutes. Baked fruit turnovers take forever, but turnover-like Grilled Goat Cheese & Nectarine Sandwiches made in a frying pan become crisp and golden in 5 to 7 minutes.

To save time, I tried other unconventional cooking methods, like making Rocky Road Brownies and Maple Caramel Baked Apples in the microwave and Peanut Butter Cup S'Mores in the broiler. Strawberries with Warm Rhubarb Sauce & Amaretti® was designed to resemble an oven-baked crisp, although it never goes near an oven. Instead, it consists of uncooked strawberries topped with sweetened stewed rhubarb and sprinkled with crisp crushed cookies.

Use Convenient Ingredients

I have never used a commercial pie crust, a box of instant pudding, or a tub of nondairy whipped topping in my desserts. The artificial and inferior flavors these products bring to any dessert cancel out any time-saving benefits gained. There are, however, a number of convenient ingredients with integrity that do give my recipes a jumpstart. Here are my favorites:

CHOCOLATE: For chocoholics, chocolate eaten out of hand is the ultimate quick dessert. But its versatility in helping to create new desserts is unparalleled. Melted, it can coat small bunches of grapes; combined with peanut butter it becomes an outstanding sundae sauce; whisked with some heavy cream and a little bit of brandy it is a fondue; let the ganache thicken and you can use it to sandwich two cookies together; chocolate puddings and mousses are so simple to make and always crowd-pleasers. There isn't a chapter in this book that doesn't contain a selection of chocolate desserts.

WHIPPED CREAM: Like chocolate, a whipped cream garnish is sometimes all you need to transform a basic ingredient or simple dessert item into a real dessert. I use it to frost simple cakes, to layer with fruit and shortcakes, to fold together with fruit purée to make a fruit fool, to top a banana split or a sundae, and in so many other ways. Avoid commercial whipped cream in a can. It never has the same fresh taste as homemade whipped cream. Instead, take a minute or two to combine heavy cream in the mixer with sugar to taste (I like 1 cup cream with 2 tablespoons sugar), and whip it until it just holds stiff peaks. Don't overwhip it, or it will become grainy and eventually separate.

COOKIES: Not only do I dress up store-bought cookies by sandwiching them with buttercream or dipping them in chocolate, I use ladyfingers to garnish a Mascarpone Mousse or crumbled butter waffle cookies to layer with ice cream and berries for Butter Waffle Ice Cream Parfaits. There are plenty of tasty choices on the supermarket shelves. If you base your dessert on ready-made cookies, you'll be several steps ahead before you even begin to cook.

UNUSUAL DOUGHS: I love to find quick alternatives to traditional pastry doughs. Frozen pizza dough is great for making rustic fruit tarts. Tortillas can stand in for crepes and can even be transformed into quick cookies. Phyllo dough is crisp and flaky like puff pastry, but it bakes up much more quickly.

INSTANT GRAINS: Unlike instant chocolate or butterscotch puddings, which are loaded with sugar and artificial colorings and flavorings, instant tapioca and couscous are unadulterated grains that simply cook very quickly. Add your own cream, sugar, and other flavoring ingredients and you can have a luscious pudding dessert on the table in 15 minutes or less. Use the recipes I have here as guides to improvise your own versions.

✳ STAYING ON TRACK ✳

To reach your dessert destination on time, you can't let yourself get sidetracked. Here are some tips to help you work purposefully toward your goal. They may seem obvious, but I write from bitter experience when I warn you to ignore them at your own risk.

Get Organized
Before you actually begin to cook, take a moment to make sure you have all of the ingredients and equipment that you will need. It is better to realize at this point that you only have one egg in the refrigerator when the recipe for Baked Apple-Raspberry Pancake calls for three than to get to the point where you are ready to add the eggs, and suffer that heartbreak.

Read the Recipe
You wouldn't hop into your car and start to drive someplace you've never been to before without first studying the directions or consulting a map. Even the simplest recipes can have unexpected twists and turns, so prepare yourself by looking ahead. For example, you need to know that the pan that will hold the Milk Chocolate, Peanut & Raisin Bark should be popped

into the freezer while the chocolate is melting, so that the chocolate will set up quickly when it comes in contact with the cold metal. You should also know that the peanuts should be chopped before the chocolate is poured into the pan. If you have to chop the peanuts after you've already poured the chocolate into the ice-cold pan, the chocolate may very well harden before you have time to sprinkle the peanuts on top of it.

Slow Down

It may seem counterintuitive, but you are less likely to finish on time when you start off in a hurry. If you skip right to mixing the batter for your Rosemary-Orange Mini Cupcakes without first preheating the oven, you will then have to twiddle your thumbs while the oven reaches 350 degrees and your batter sits in the bowl. If you forget to line a baking sheet with parchment before dipping your apples into melted caramel, you will be scrambling to find a nonstick surface to set it down on, reaching for the parchment in the drawer while holding the apple suspended over the pot. Backtracking like this always costs you minutes in the end. So take a deep breath and work deliberately from start to finish instead of rushing headlong into a recipe.

✳ DESTINATION: QUICK DESSERT ✳

Every day for the last several months I took a different route to dessert, exploring the many possible paths to something simple and sweet. Occasionally, there was a roadblock (a deconstructed chocolate bread pudding just couldn't be done within the allotted time) or an unexpected delay (I spent 10 minutes making that first batch of Sesame & Honey Candy and 40 minutes peeling it off of the ungreased foil). But now I know 100 ways to make a 30-minute dessert, and I'm pleased to share these shortcuts with you. I hope that they will allow you to enjoy something sweet as often as you like, and give you an excuse to linger a few extra minutes at the end of each meal (at the table) with your friends and family.

Chapter 1

Quick COOKIES

*During the course of my career, I've written dozens of cookie recipes and baked thousands of cookies. I've employed some great time-*saving tricks, like melting butter instead of waiting for it to soften (I haven't noticed any difference in my peanut butter cookies), and freezing unbaked balls of dough so I can have fresh oatmeal cookies in the time it takes to heat the oven and bake them off. But even an experienced, efficient, and organized baker like myself couldn't get a batch of cookies mixed, baked, and served in 30 minutes using conventional methods. Individual cookies must be portioned out onto cookie sheets that can only hold twelve cookies each, and each batch requires at least 10 minutes to bake. Do the math, and you will see that baking time alone for 36 chocolate chip cookies will be 30 minutes. Bar cookies can be baked in a single batch, but a pan of brownies or blondies requires at least 30 minutes in the oven, leaving no time for gathering ingredients and mixing.

So for the cookie recipes in this book, I turned to unconventional ingredients. I scoured the supermarket shelves for cookies I could dress up with homemade frostings and fillings. Covering imported all-butter shortbread fingers with best-quality dark chocolate takes just minutes, leaving time to decorate them with dots of white chocolate to resemble dominoes. To make Mallomar®-type cookies at home, place dollops of Marshmallow Fluff® on wheatmeal biscuits, then pour some melted chocolate on top. Put them in the refrigerator for a few minutes and they're ready to eat.

Sandwich cookies are simple to make with store-bought cookies, and the combinations you can create are endless. I like thin gingersnaps filled with milk chocolate ganache or delicate almond thins stuck together with orange-flavored buttercream. Then there are open-faced sandwiches. Vanilla wafers topped with sweetened cream cheese and a single berry make very pretty cheesecake petits fours. Belgian waffle cookies heated for a few minutes in the oven become soft and fragrant, the perfect crust for little mascarpone and strawberry tarts. I've included a scrumptious variation on the s'more made with chocolate wafer cookies, Marshmallow Fluff, and a Reese's® Peanut Butter Cup®—they can be put together in the time it takes to heat your broiler.

I also experimented with some unconventional techniques to produce fresh-baked cookies in less than half an hour. Instead of making dough from scratch for crisp and caramelized cinnamon wafers, I use a biscuit cutter to cut large flour tortillas into small rounds, then brush them with butter and coat them with cinnamon sugar before baking briefly. They're perfect with hot chocolate.

There are several great ways to produce fantastic homemade cookies quickly without using the oven. I've been making brownies in the microwave for years, and the Rocky Road version I include here is my most decadent recipe yet. Baking oatmeal–chocolate chip cookies in a waffle iron instead of the oven cuts down considerably on baking time. These pretty cookies take about 2 minutes to bake, as opposed to 10 minutes in the oven.

Finally, don't overlook deep-frying if you want to produce cookies in a flash. Cloudlike ricotta fritters, surprisingly elegant and absolutely irresistible when dusted with powdered sugar and drizzled with maple syrup, can be on the table in well under 30 minutes.

Almond Thin Sandwiches

WITH ORANGE CARDAMOM CREAM

I am a big fan of butter cookies made in Belgium, and particularly of the thin and delicate almond wafers from Jules Destrooper®. Almonds combine naturally with orange and cardamom, so I make a simple flavored buttercream and sandwich them together.

1. In a medium bowl, cream the confectioners' sugar and butter with a fork until the mixture resembles coarse meal. Add the orange zest and juice and cardamom and continue to cream until smooth and soft.

2. Use a small metal spatula to spread a thin layer of orange-cardamom cream over half of the cookies. Top with the remaining cookies. Serve immediately or store in an airtight container in the refrigerator for up to 6 hours and bring to room temperature before serving.

Makes 14

¼ CUP CONFECTIONERS' SUGAR

1 TABLESPOON UNSALTED BUTTER, SOFTENED

¼ TEASPOON FINELY GRATED ORANGE ZEST

1½ TEASPOONS ORANGE JUICE

⅛ TEASPOON GROUND CARDAMOM

28 ALMOND THIN COOKIES

Sandwich Cookies

I love the combination of ginger and milk chocolate, so sandwiching milk chocolate ganache between delicate gingersnaps was a no-brainer for me. Be sure to use thin Swedish-style cookies—thicker gingersnaps are too bulky and hard for sandwiching. To make these in under 30 minutes, use an ice bath to cool off your ganache. But don't let it get too cold (3 to 5 minutes should be long enough) or it will be difficult to spread.

1. Combine the chocolate and heavy cream in a small microwave-safe bowl. Melt the chocolate in the microwave on high, 30 seconds to 1 minute, depending on the power and size of your microwave. Stir until smooth.

2. Set the bowl of chocolate over a larger bowl of ice and let stand, whisking occasionally, until thick but spreadable, about 5 minutes.

3. Use a small metal spatula to spread a heaping teaspoon of ganache onto the flat side of a cookie and top with another cookie. Repeat with the remaining ganache and cookies. Serve immediately or store in an airtight container at room temperature for up to 1 day before serving.

Makes 15

4 OUNCES MILK CHOCOLATE, FINELY CHOPPED

1/4 CUP HEAVY CREAM

30 THIN SWEDISH-STYLE GINGERSNAP COOKIES (ONE 5.25-OUNCE PACKAGE)

MIX-AND-MATCH SANDWICH COOKIES

Simple buttercream filling, made with 1 tablespoon butter with ¼ cup confectioners' sugar, can be flavored in a variety of ways, and sandwiched between a large selection of cookies to suit your taste. Customize your cookies by adding a flavoring ingredient from Column A to your buttercream to fill a sandwich made with supermarket cookies from Column B.

A

¼ TEASPOON VANILLA EXTRACT AND 1½ TEASPOONS MILK OR HEAVY CREAM

¼ TEASPOON FINELY GRATED LEMON ZEST AND 1 TEASPOON LEMON JUICE

¼ TEASPOON MAPLE EXTRACT AND 1½ TEASPOONS PURE MAPLE SYRUP

¼ TEASPOON ALMOND EXTRACT AND 1½ TEASPOONS MILK

¼ TEASPOON VANILLA EXTRACT, 1½ TEASPOONS MILK OR HEAVY CREAM, AND 1 TABLESPOON MINI CHOCOLATE CHIPS

⅛ TEASPOON GROUND CINNAMON, ⅛ TEASPOON GROUND GINGER, PINCH OF GROUND NUTMEG, AND 1½ TEASPOONS MILK OR HEAVY CREAM

¼ TEASPOON COCONUT EXTRACT, 1 TABLESPOON SWEETENED FLAKED COCONUT, AND 1½ TEASPOONS MILK OR HEAVY CREAM

B

NABISCO® FAMOUS CHOCOLATE WAFERS

NEWMAN'S OWN® ALPHABET COOKIES

JULES DESTROOPER APPLE THINS

PLANTERS'® PEANUT BUTTER COOKIE CRISPS

MINI CHIPS AHOY®

AMARETTI COOKIE SNAPS

NORFOLK MANOR LEMON BISCUITS

Chocolate Marshmallow Cookies

*These homemade Mallomar-type cookies are easy to make and far superior
to the supermarket variety. I like Carr's® Whole Wheat Biscuits, which are basically
round graham crackers, but you can use any round, not-too-sweet cookie that you like in
combination with marshmallow and chocolate. Freezing the cookies before coating them
with the chocolate helps the Fluff keep its shape. Be sure to coat them completely with
chocolate, so none of the Fluff oozes out.*

1. Put the biscuits on a wire rack set over a rimmed baking sheet. Top each biscuit with a rounded heaping tablespoonful of Fluff. Place the baking sheet in the freezer for 10 minutes to firm up.

2. Combine the chocolate and oil in a medium microwave-safe bowl. Melt the chocolate in the microwave on high for 1 to 2 minutes, depending on the power and size of your microwave. Stir until smooth. Spoon some chocolate over each biscuit to coat completely.

3. Return the baking sheet to the freezer for another 10 minutes, until the chocolate is set. Refrigerate for up to 6 hours, until ready to serve.

Makes 12

12 CARR'S WHOLE WHEAT BISCUITS

1½ CUPS MARSHMALLOW FLUFF

8 OUNCES BEST-QUALITY BITTERSWEET CHOCOLATE, FINELY CHOPPED

2 TABLESPOONS VEGETABLE OIL

CHOCOLATE-COVERED

Shortbread Dominoes

*Walkers® Pure Butter Shortbread, made in Scotland with just flour, butter,
sugar, and salt, is one of the treasures of the supermarket. These shortbread fingers, dipped
in premium chocolate and decorated to look like dominoes, are transformed into dessert-
quality cookies for casual entertaining.*

1. Put the cookies on a wire rack set over a rimmed baking sheet.
2. Combine the chocolate and oil in a small microwave-safe bowl. Melt the chocolate in the microwave on high for 30 seconds to 1 minute, depending on the power and size of your microwave. Stir until smooth. Spoon some chocolate over each cookie and use a small metal spatula to completely cover the top and sides. Put the baking sheet in the freezer until the chocolate is firm, 5 to 10 minutes.
3. Meanwhile, put the white chocolate in another small microwave-safe bowl. Melt it in the microwave on high for 30 seconds. Stir until smooth. Dip a skewer in the melted white chocolate and draw a line across each cookie once the dark chocolate is firm. Add domino dots on each side of the line. (Alternatively, you can use a pastry bag fitted with a small plain tip or scrape the white chocolate into a small zip-top plastic bag, cut a very small hole in one corner of the bag, and squeeze the chocolate onto the cookies.)
4. Return the baking sheet to the freezer for another 5 minutes until the white chocolate is set, or refrigerate for up to 6 hours before ready to serve.

Makes 8

8 WALKERS PURE BUTTER SHORTBREAD COOKIES

4 OUNCES BEST-QUALITY BITTERSWEET CHOCOLATE, FINELY CHOPPED

2 TEASPOONS VEGETABLE OIL

1 OUNCE WHITE CHOCOLATE, FINELY CHOPPED

Peanut Butter Cup S'Mores

Browned Marshmallow Fluff and a melting Reese's Peanut Butter Cup smushed between two chocolate wafer cookies makes an absolutely sensational variation on the s'more. Substitute large marshmallows for the Fluff if you like, and adjust the broiling time since they may take a few seconds longer to brown.

1. Preheat the broiler to high. Set an oven rack as close to the heating element as possible.
2. Arrange 6 of the cookies on a baking sheet. Top each one with a peanut butter cup and then 1 tablespoon of the Fluff. Broil until the marshmallow is bubbling and golden brown, about 30 seconds.
3. Remove the baking sheet from the oven, top each s'more with a cookie, pressing down lightly, and serve immediately.

Makes 6

12 CHOCOLATE WAFER COOKIES

6 LARGE REESE'S PEANUT BUTTER CUPS

6 TABLESPOONS MARSHMALLOW FLUFF

VANILLA WAFER

Cheesecake Tarts

Here is a minimalist approach to cheesecake: Pretty little petit four–type tarts made by simply spooning a little sweetened cream cheese on top of a Nilla wafer and garnishing with a fresh berry.

1. Combine the cream cheese, lemon juice and zest, and vanilla in a medium bowl and beat with an electric mixer until very smooth. Beat in the confectioners' sugar.

2. Arrange the vanilla wafers on a serving platter. Spoon a heaping tablespoon of the cream cheese mixture on each one, then top with a berry. Garnish the platter with mint leaves. Serve immediately, or refrigerate for up to 1 hour before serving.

Makes 12

4 OUNCES CREAM CHEESE, SOFTENED

1 TABLESPOON FRESH LEMON JUICE

½ TEASPOON FINELY GRATED LEMON ZEST

¼ TEASPOON VANILLA EXTRACT

3 TABLESPOONS CONFECTIONERS' SUGAR

12 VANILLA WAFERS

12 FRESH RASPBERRIES OR BLACKBERRIES

SMALL FRESH MINT LEAVES FOR GARNISH

Butter Waffle Tarts

*These buttery cookies get soft and flexible when warmed in the oven,
so when you spread them with some sweetened mascarpone and top with
macerated strawberries, you get the effect of just-baked tarts.*

1. Preheat the oven to 300 degrees. Arrange the cookies on a baking sheet.

2. Combine the strawberries and 2 teaspoons of the sugar in a small bowl and let stand, stirring occasionally, until the sugar is dissolved, about 10 minutes.

3. Meanwhile, combine the mascarpone, the remaining 1 teaspoon sugar, and the vanilla in another small bowl and stir to combine.

4. Bake the cookies until warmed, about 5 minutes. Spread each one with some of the mascarpone, spoon the strawberries on top, and serve immediately.

Makes 4

4 BELGIAN BUTTER WAFFLE COOKIES, SUCH AS JULES DESTROOPER

I CUP HULLED AND SLICED FRESH STRAWBERRIES (ABOUT 6 MEDIUM)

I TABLESPOON GRANULATED SUGAR

½ CUP MASCARPONE, SOFTENED

½ TEASPOON VANILLA EXTRACT

Microwave Brownies

These gooey brownies are great on their own, or you can use them to build brownie ice cream sundaes, by putting the warm squares in sundae dishes and topping with coffee ice cream, whipped cream, and a maraschino cherry.

1. Coat the bottom and sides of an 8-inch-square microwave-safe baking dish with nonstick cooking spray.
2. Put the butter and cocoa in a large microwave-safe bowl, cover with plastic wrap, and microwave on high until the butter is melted, 30 seconds to 1 minute, depending on the power and size of your oven.
3. Add the sugar and stir to combine. Whisk in the eggs and vanilla. Stir in the flour, then the chocolate chips, marshmallows, and nuts. Scrape the batter into the prepared baking dish. Microwave on high until the brownies are just set in the center, 4 to 7 minutes.
4. Let the brownies cool in the pan on a wire rack for 10 minutes, then cut into 16 squares and serve immediately.

Makes 16

NONSTICK COOKING SPRAY

1/2 CUP (1 STICK) UNSALTED BUTTER, CUT INTO 8 PIECES

3/4 CUP UNSWEETENED DUTCH-PROCESS COCOA POWDER

1 1/2 CUPS GRANULATED SUGAR

3 LARGE EGGS

1 TEASPOON VANILLA EXTRACT

3/4 CUP UNBLEACHED ALL-PURPOSE FLOUR

1 CUP MILK CHOCOLATE CHIPS

3/4 CUP MINI MARSHMALLOWS

3/4 CUP CHOPPED WALNUTS OR PECANS

Warm Cinnamon Crisps

WITH HOT CHOCOLATE

If you like the Mexican combination of churros y chocolate, *this is the dessert for you.*
Flour tortillas cut into small rounds and glazed with cinnamon sugar puff up
and get caramelized and crispy in the oven. They are a delicious accompaniment
to hot chocolate enriched with cream.

1. Preheat the oven to 500 degrees. Use a biscuit cutter to cut the tortillas into sixteen 2½-inch rounds. Combine the sugar and cinnamon in a small bowl.

2. Put the butter on a rimmed baking sheet and put the baking sheet in the oven until the butter is melted, 1 to 2 minutes. Remove the sheet from the oven and spread the tortilla rounds on the sheet, turning to coat both sides in the butter. Sprinkle the tops with the cinnamon sugar and return to the oven. Bake until the rounds are golden, 3 to 5 minutes. Transfer to a paper towel–lined baking sheet to cool slightly.

3. Combine the milk and heavy cream in a medium saucepan and bring to a boil over medium-high heat. Reduce the heat to low and whisk in the chocolate until melted. Whisk in the vanilla. Pour into mugs and serve with the warm cinnamon crisps on the side.

Serves 4

TWO 9- TO 10-INCH FLOUR TORTILLAS

2 TABLESPOONS GRANULATED SUGAR

¼ TEASPOON GROUND CINNAMON

¼ CUP (½ STICK) UNSALTED BUTTER, CUT INTO PIECES

3 CUPS WHOLE OR 2% MILK

1 CUP HEAVY CREAM

6 OUNCES SEMISWEET CHOCOLATE, FINELY CHOPPED

½ TEASPOON VANILLA EXTRACT

Fig Shortbread Bites

Buttery and perfumed with vanilla, these little cookies are much better than store-bought fig cookies. They take less than 10 minutes to bake in a mini muffin tin.

1. Preheat the oven to 375 degrees. Coat a 12-cup mini muffin tin with nonstick cooking spray.
2. Combine the flour, baking powder, and salt in a small bowl.
3. Combine the butter and granulated sugar in a medium bowl and cream with an electric mixer until smooth. Stir in the egg yolk, then the vanilla. Stir in the flour mixture.
4. Divide the dough in half. Take one half of it and divide it evenly between the 12 muffin cups, smoothing it with a spoon to cover the bottom of each cup evenly. Spoon ½ teaspoon of the jam into each cup. Spoon the remaining dough on top of the jam and smooth.
5. Bake until the tops of the cookies are golden, 13 to 15 minutes. Remove from the oven and invert the tin onto a wire rack. Serve warm, dusted with confectioners' sugar if desired, or let cool completely on the rack and store in an airtight container for up to 3 days before dusting with the sugar and serving.

Makes 12

NONSTICK COOKING SPRAY

½ CUP UNBLEACHED ALL-PURPOSE FLOUR

¼ TEASPOON BAKING POWDER

PINCH OF SALT

¼ CUP (½ STICK) UNSALTED BUTTER, SOFTENED

¼ CUP GRANULATED SUGAR

1 LARGE EGG YOLK

½ TEASPOON VANILLA EXTRACT

1½ TABLESPOONS FIG JAM

2 TEASPOONS CONFECTIONERS' SUGAR (OPTIONAL)

Ricotta Fritters

WITH MAPLE SYRUP

*I never really considered deep-frying as a dessert shortcut until I had some ricotta fritters
at a wonderful Italian restaurant in New York City. But when I thought about
how quick the batter must be to make, and how cooking only took a few minutes,
I had to try them at home. Here I pour a little maple syrup on dessert plates and set the
hot fritters on top, although you could simply sweeten them with confectioners' sugar
or dip them in honey or even chocolate syrup instead.*

1. Heat 2 inches of vegetable oil in a large saucepan over medium-high heat. Line a baking sheet with paper towels.
2. Whisk the egg, sugar, ricotta, and vanilla in a medium bowl. Whisk in the flour and salt.
3. Carefully drop 6 individual tablespoonfuls of batter into the hot oil (test the oil by dropping a little bit of batter into it; it should bubble up—if it doesn't, let the oil heat some more). Fry, turning once, until the fritters are golden brown on both sides, 2 to 3 minutes total. Use a slotted spoon to transfer the fritters to the baking sheet to drain. Repeat with the remaining batter.
4. Drizzle 2 tablespoons maple syrup on each of 4 dessert plates. Dust the fritters heavily with confectioners' sugar, arrange them on top of the maple syrup, and serve immediately.

Makes about 12

VEGETABLE OIL FOR FRYING

I LARGE EGG

3 TABLESPOONS GRANULATED SUGAR

1/2 CUP WHOLE-MILK RICOTTA

1/2 TEASPOON VANILLA EXTRACT

1/3 CUP UNBLEACHED ALL-PURPOSE FLOUR

PINCH OF SALT

1/2 CUP PURE MAPLE SYRUP

CONFECTIONERS' SUGAR FOR DUSTING

Waffle Cookies

Baking cookie dough in a waffle iron takes about a minute and a half, a real time-saver when you've got to have warm cookies right away. Although they look like mini waffles, they bake up just like cookies, and after they cool they'll keep in an airtight container for several days, just like conventional cookies. Once cooled, they look cute garnishing bowls of ice cream. I like oatmeal and chocolate chip waffle cookies, because the oats become browned and toasty on the outside and the chips are all gooey and melty, but you can substitute raisins or chopped dates for the chips and add ¼ teaspoon ground cinnamon and a pinch of nutmeg for a more classic oatmeal cookie flavor.

1. Heat the waffle iron according to the manufacturer's instructions.
2. In a large bowl, whisk the butter and brown sugar until smooth. Whisk in the eggs and vanilla. Stir in the flour, baking soda, and salt. Stir in the oats and chocolate chips.
3. Coat the grids of the waffle iron with nonstick cooking spray. Use a tablespoon or small ice cream scoop to portion out a cookie onto each waffle square. Close the iron and cook until set and beginning to brown, 1½ to 3 minutes, depending on the heat of your waffle iron. Use a thin metal spatula to transfer the cooked cookies to a wire rack and repeat with the remaining dough, coating the grids with spray as necessary. The cookies will keep at room temperature in an airtight container for 2 to 3 days.

Makes 24

½ CUP (1 STICK) UNSALTED BUTTER, MELTED

½ CUP PLUS 2 TABLESPOONS FIRMLY PACKED LIGHT BROWN SUGAR

2 LARGE EGGS

1 TEASPOON VANILLA EXTRACT

¾ CUP UNBLEACHED ALL-PURPOSE FLOUR

½ TEASPOON BAKING SODA

¼ TEASPOON SALT

1½ CUPS OLD-FASHIONED ROLLED OATS (NOT INSTANT)

1 CUP SEMISWEET CHOCOLATE CHIPS

NONSTICK COOKING SPRAY

Chapter 2

Cake WALK

Look at the simplest cake recipes in the world—plain pound cake, cheesecake, one-bowl chocolate buttermilk cake—and you'll see that no matter how short the ingredient lists, how easy the techniques, how basic the embellishments, there is no way you'll be able to get one on the table in 30 minutes. Most cakes must bake for at least that long, and usually much longer, before they're cooked through.

Dividing your batter into small portions and making miniature cakes is the obvious solution to this problem. Tiny cakes baked in madeleine pans, muffin tins, mini Bundt pans, and ramekins are done in a fraction of the time that a larger cake takes to bake. This chapter contains recipes for a wide variety of cakes, from tender Gingerbread Madeleines to Rosemary-Orange Mini Cupcakes to Fresh Blueberry Upside-Down Cakes, none of which bake for more than 20 minutes.

When I'm making small cakes, I'll often go for an over-the-top richness, sweetness, gooey texture, or bold flavor that I wouldn't try with a bigger cake. Cupcakes loaded with almond paste to make them extra dense and moist, molten chocolate cakes with a jolt of cayenne pepper, creamy little goat cheese cakes—these desserts are just right in mini portions. Also wonderful in small sizes are cakes so tender that they might fall apart if baked in bigger pans—madeleines are in this category, as are the Cinnamon Bundt Cakes made with cake flour so they're extra soft.

To save time, I keep frostings and fillings simple. The cake embellishments in this chapter, from the teaspoonful of crème fraîche that top the Rosemary-Orange Mini Cupcakes to the Espresso Cream Glaze that covers the Mini Walnut Layer Cakes, can be assembled while the cakes are baking.

If you want to satisfy your craving for cake without turning on your oven, there is a way: Bake your cake batter in a waffle iron. I adapted two favorite cake recipes for the waffle iron. The results, Sour Cream & Pecan Waffles and Milk Chocolate Brownie Waffles, are delicious warm from the waffle iron, either on their own or topped with ice cream. Cheddar Waffles with Pears & Honey were inspired by the classic autumn dessert combination of apple pie and Cheddar cheese.

The chapter ends with two recipes for large cakes that, amazingly, can be put together and baked in under 30 minutes. One is Baked Apple & Raspberry Pancake. Yes, pancakes are cakes, too! The batter is mixed in a food processor, poured into a pan of sautéed apples and berries, and baked in a very hot oven for just 15 minutes. The other, an ethereal Lemon Soufflé Omelet, takes just 10 minutes to rise. Either one makes a beautiful brunch dish or a special but unfussy dinner party dessert.

Gingerbread Madeleines

As I tried to think of cake recipes that could be ready in 30 minutes, I remembered how quick buttery madeleines were to put together. Could other cake batters be baked in a madeleine pan? It was winter, so I adapted a favorite gingerbread cake recipe and was very happy with the spicy but comforting little cakes that were the result. Sprinkle them with cinnamon sugar hot out of the oven, or serve them with some sweetened whipped cream with a little ground cinnamon if you'd like.

1. Preheat the oven to 375 degrees. Grease a 12-cavity madeleine pan with butter.

2. Stir the hot water, molasses, and baking soda in a small bowl. Set aside.

3. Combine the softened butter, brown sugar, salt, ginger, and cinnamon in a medium bowl and beat with an electric mixer until smooth. Add the egg yolk and beat until well incorporated. Stir in the molasses mixture. Stir in the baking powder, then the flour. Spoon the batter into the cavities.

4. Bake until the madeleines are well risen and golden, 9 to 10 minutes. Remove the pan from the oven and immediately invert onto a wire rack to cool. Serve warm or at room temperature. These are best eaten the day they are baked.

Makes 12

BUTTER FOR GREASING THE PAN

6 TABLESPOONS VERY HOT TAP WATER

¼ CUP DARK MOLASSES

½ TEASPOON BAKING SODA

2 TABLESPOONS UNSALTED BUTTER, SOFTENED

¼ CUP FIRMLY PACKED LIGHT BROWN SUGAR

PINCH OF SALT

¾ TEASPOON GROUND GINGER

¼ TEASPOON GROUND CINNAMON

1 LARGE EGG YOLK

1 TEASPOON BAKING POWDER

½ CUP PLUS 2 TABLESPOONS UNBLEACHED ALL-PURPOSE FLOUR

Lemon-Cornmeal Madeleines

Cake flour is essential here if you want delicate little cakes with a cornmeal crunch.
Vary the recipe by substituting orange zest for the lemon, and/or adding ½ teaspoon finely
chopped fresh thyme or ¼ teaspoon finely chopped fresh rosemary.

1. Preheat the oven to 375 degrees. Grease a 12-cavity madeleine pan with butter.
2. In a large bowl, whisk the whole egg, egg yolk, granulated sugar, lemon zest, vanilla, and salt until well blended, about 1 minute. Gently fold in the flour, cornmeal, and baking powder with a rubber spatula until just incorporated. Fold in the melted butter. Spoon the batter into the cavities.
3. Bake until the madeleines are well risen and golden, about 10 minutes. Remove the pan from the oven and immediately invert onto a wire rack to cool. Serve warm or at room temperature, dusting with confectioners' sugar, if desired, just before serving. These are best eaten the day they are baked.

Makes 12

BUTTER FOR GREASING THE PAN

1 LARGE EGG

1 LARGE EGG YOLK

6 TABLESPOONS GRANULATED SUGAR

1½ TEASPOONS FINELY GRATED LEMON ZEST

1 TEASPOON VANILLA EXTRACT

⅛ TEASPOON SALT

6 TABLESPOONS CAKE FLOUR

6 TABLESPOONS YELLOW CORNMEAL

1½ TEASPOONS BAKING POWDER

6 TABLESPOONS (¾ STICK) UNSALTED BUTTER, MELTED AND COOLED

CONFECTIONERS' SUGAR FOR DUSTING (OPTIONAL)

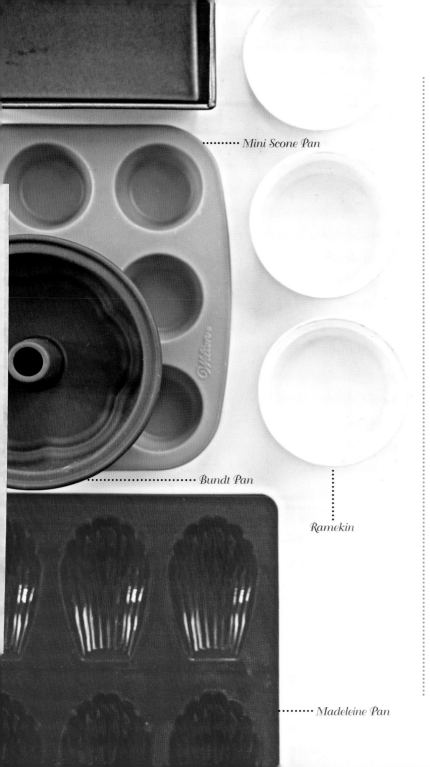

Mini Scone Pan

Bundt Pan

Ramekin

Madeleine Pan

BEYOND MUFFIN TINS

Mini Bakeware for Quick Cakes and Other Baked Goods

If you don't yet own a madeleine pan, a muffin tin, or a set of small ceramic ramekins, you can pick them up in the baking aisle of your supermarket or any cookware shop. But once you see how simple these small cakes are to make, you may become obsessed with owning small size pans of every shape—shallow crème brûlée dishes, mini scone and loaf pans, tiny pie plates, doughnut, shortcake, and crumb cake pans—the better to experiment with quick mini cakes. This has been my experience, and I now have an entire cabinet devoted to mini bakeware, much of it ordered from The Baker's Catalog (www.kingarthurflour.com). The experts at King Arthur® have conveniently gathered these items into a mini bakeware section of their online catalog. So far I have been able to resist the temptations of the mini hamburger bun pan and the mini popover pan, but I don't know how much longer I can hold out.

Cocoa Madeleines

Cocoa powder tends to clump up, so be sure to sift it through a fine strainer right into the mixing bowl before folding it into the egg mixture. Use Dutch-process cocoa for a rich flavor.

1. Preheat the oven to 375 degrees. Grease a 12-cavity madeleine pan with butter.

2. In a large bowl, whisk the whole egg, egg yolk, granulated sugar, vanilla, and salt until well blended, about 1 minute. Sift the cocoa into the bowl. Add the flour and baking powder and gently fold with a rubber spatula until just incorporated. Fold in the melted butter. Spoon the batter into the cavities.

3. Bake until the madeleines are well risen and firm, about 10 minutes. Remove the pan from the oven and immediately invert onto a wire rack to cool. Serve warm or at room temperature, dusting with confectioners' sugar, if desired, just before serving. These are best eaten the day they are baked.

Makes 12

BUTTER FOR GREASING THE PAN

1 LARGE EGG

1 LARGE EGG YOLK

6 TABLESPOONS GRANULATED SUGAR

1 TEASPOON VANILLA EXTRACT

1/8 TEASPOON SALT

1/4 CUP UNSWEETENED DUTCH-PROCESS COCOA POWDER

1/2 CUP UNBLEACHED ALL-PURPOSE FLOUR

1 1/2 TEASPOONS BAKING POWDER

6 TABLESPOONS (3/4 STICK) UNSALTED BUTTER, MELTED AND COOLED

CONFECTIONERS' SUGAR FOR DUSTING (OPTIONAL)

Buttery Almond Madeleines

The first time I made these wonderful madeleines, they filled the kitchen with an intoxicating aroma and were devoured before they were out of the oven for 5 minutes.

1. Preheat the oven to 375 degrees. Grease a 12-cavity madeleine pan with butter.

2. In a large bowl, whisk the whole egg, egg yolk, granulated sugar, almond extract, and salt until well blended, about 1 minute. Gently fold in the flour, ground almonds, and baking powder with a rubber spatula until just incorporated. Fold in the melted butter. Spoon the batter into the cavities.

3. Bake until the madeleines are well risen and golden, about 10 minutes. Remove the pan from the oven and immediately invert onto a wire rack to cool. Serve warm or at room temperature, dusting with confectioners' sugar, if desired, just before serving. These are best eaten the day they are baked.

Makes 12

BUTTER FOR GREASING THE PAN

1 LARGE EGG

1 LARGE EGG YOLK

6 TABLESPOONS GRANULATED SUGAR

1/2 TEASPOON ALMOND EXTRACT

1/8 TEASPOON SALT

3/4 CUP UNBLEACHED ALL-PURPOSE FLOUR

1/4 CUP SLICED BLANCHED ALMONDS, FINELY GROUND IN A FOOD PROCESSOR

1 1/2 TEASPOONS BAKING POWDER

6 TABLESPOONS (3/4 STICK) UNSALTED BUTTER, MELTED AND COOLED

CONFECTIONERS' SUGAR FOR DUSTING (OPTIONAL)

Mini Cupcakes

Enjoy these fragrant little cupcakes warm from the oven. A teaspoon of crème fraîche is all that's needed to frost them. No need to sweeten the cream — its tartness complements the caramel sweetness of the brown sugar in the cakes.

1. Preheat the oven to 350 degrees. Grease a 24-cup mini muffin tin with butter.

2. In a large bowl, cream the ½ cup butter and the brown sugar with an electric mixer until fluffy, about 3 minutes, scraping down the sides of the bowl once or twice as necessary. Add the eggs, rosemary, and orange zest and beat, scraping down the bowl once, until well combined. Add the flour, baking powder, and salt and mix on low until just combined.

3. Spoon the batter into the muffin tin and bake until the tops of the cupcakes are just golden, about 10 minutes. Remove the pan from the oven, immediately invert onto a wire rack, and let cool for 5 minutes. Serve warm or at room temperature, topping each cupcake with a teaspoon of crème fraîche, if desired.

Makes 24

½ CUP (1 STICK) UNSALTED BUTTER, SOFTENED; PLUS MORE FOR GREASING THE PAN

½ CUP PLUS 2 TABLESPOONS FIRMLY PACKED LIGHT BROWN SUGAR

2 LARGE EGGS

1 TEASPOON FINELY CHOPPED FRESH ROSEMARY

1 TEASPOON FINELY GRATED ORANGE ZEST

¾ CUP UNBLEACHED ALL-PURPOSE FLOUR

½ TEASPOON BAKING POWDER

⅛ TEASPOON SALT

½ CUP CRÈME FRAÎCHE (OPTIONAL)

Mini Walnut Layer Cakes

WITH ESPRESSO CREAM FILLING & GLAZE

Once long ago, my mother gave me a "muffin top" pan, and I've finally found a use for it. Cake batter bakes amazingly quickly in the shallow cavities, and sandwiching two of the cakes together creates a charming mini layer cake effect. (Muffin top pans have 6 cavities, just like muffin tins.) Here, I use a batter enriched with ground walnuts, the flavor of which is enhanced by a strong but sweet espresso cream filling and glaze.

1. Preheat the oven to 350 degrees. Coat two 6-cavity muffin top tins with nonstick cooking spray.

2. In a large bowl, cream the butter and brown sugar with an electric mixer until fluffy, about 3 minutes, scraping down the sides of the bowl once or twice as necessary. Add the eggs and vanilla and beat, scraping down the bowl once, until well combined. Add the flour, ground walnuts, baking powder, and salt and mix on low until just combined. Spoon the batter into the muffin top tins and smooth to the edges of each cavity with a spatula.

3. Bake until the tops of the layers are just golden, about 10 minutes. Remove the pan from the oven and immediately invert onto a wire rack. Let cool for 10 minutes.

4. While the layers are cooling, make the glaze: Whisk the confectioners' sugar, heavy cream, and espresso powder in a medium bowl until smooth. Smooth some glaze on the top of the rounded side of six of the layers. Place the unglazed layers on top of the glazed layers. Smooth the remaining glaze over the tops and sides of the cakes. Top each cake with a walnut half, if you like, and serve.

Makes 3

NONSTICK COOKING SPRAY

1/2 CUP (1 STICK) UNSALTED BUTTER, SOFTENED

1/2 CUP FIRMLY PACKED LIGHT BROWN SUGAR

2 LARGE EGGS

1 1/2 TEASPOONS VANILLA EXTRACT

3/4 CUP UNBLEACHED ALL-PURPOSE FLOUR

1/2 CUP WALNUT PIECES, FINELY GROUND IN A FOOD PROCESSOR; PLUS MORE WALNUT PIECES FOR GARNISH (OPTIONAL)

1/2 TEASPOON BAKING POWDER

1/8 TEASPOON SALT

1 CUP CONFECTIONERS' SUGAR

6 TABLESPOONS HEAVY CREAM

1 TABLESPOON INSTANT ESPRESSO POWDER

German Chocolate Brownie Cakes

These little chocolate cakes look exactly like the ones my daughters make in their Easy-Bake® Oven. Even the girls admit that these taste better, especially when spread with rich cream cheese and coconut frosting.

1. Preheat the oven to 375 degrees. Coat a 6-cavity muffin top pan with nonstick cooking spray.

2. Put the butter and chocolate in a medium microwave-safe bowl and microwave on high until just melted. Stir until smooth. Whisk in the granulated sugar. Whisk in the eggs and vanilla. Stir in the flour, baking powder, and salt. Spoon the batter into the prepared pan and smooth the tops with a spatula.

3. Bake until just set, 10 to 12 minutes. Remove from the oven and let cool in the pan on a wire rack for 5 minutes. Invert onto the rack and put the layers in the freezer for 5 minutes.

4. While the layers are cooling, make the frosting. In a large bowl, cream together the cream cheese, butter, extract, and confectioners' sugar with an electric mixer until smooth, scraping down the sides of the bowl once or twice as necessary. Stir in the coconut.

5. Spread the top of each cake with some of the frosting. Serve the cakes immediately or store in an airtight container in the refrigerator for up to 1 day and bring to room temperature before serving.

Makes 6

FOR THE BROWNIE CAKES:

NONSTICK COOKING SPRAY

1/2 CUP UNSALTED BUTTER

3 OUNCES UNSWEETENED CHOCOLATE, FINELY CHOPPED

1 CUP GRANULATED SUGAR

2 LARGE EGGS

1 TEASPOON VANILLA EXTRACT

3/4 CUP UNBLEACHED ALL-PURPOSE FLOUR

1/2 TEASPOON BAKING POWDER

PINCH OF SALT

FOR THE FROSTING:

8 OUNCES CREAM CHEESE, SOFTENED

2 TABLESPOONS UNSALTED BUTTER, SOFTENED

1/4 TEASPOON COCONUT EXTRACT

3/4 CUP CONFECTIONERS' SUGAR

2 CUPS SWEETENED FLAKED COCONUT

Pudding Cakes

This is the chocolate dessert that never disappoints. Serve it and watch as your guests hungrily clean their dishes with their spoons. Don't overcook your cakes, or you won't get that molten center that makes them so irresistible. I like to spike my cakes with cinnamon and cayenne pepper to give them a little kick, but you can leave out the spices for straight-on chocolate decadence.

1. Preheat the oven to 375 degrees. Grease six 6-ounce ramekins with butter.
2. Combine the ½ cup butter and the chocolate in a small microwave-safe bowl. Melt the chocolate in the microwave on high for 30 seconds to 1 minute, depending on the power and size of your microwave. Stir until smooth. Set aside.
3. Combine the eggs and sugar in a medium bowl and beat on high with an electric mixer until pale yellow and thick, 3 to 5 minutes. Stir in the flour, salt, cinnamon, and cayenne. Stir in the chocolate mixture.
4. Spoon the batter into the prepared ramekins, arrange on a baking sheet, and bake until the cakes are firm around the edges but still loose in the center, about 12 minutes. Do not overbake. Transfer the baking sheet to a wire rack, let cool for 5 minutes, and serve.

Serves 4

½ CUP (1 STICK) UNSALTED BUTTER, CUT INTO PIECES; PLUS MORE FOR GREASING THE RAMEKINS

6 OUNCES BITTERSWEET CHOCOLATE, FINELY CHOPPED

3 LARGE EGGS

⅓ CUP GRANULATED SUGAR

¼ CUP UNBLEACHED ALL-PURPOSE FLOUR

¼ TEASPOON SALT

¼ TEASPOON GROUND CINNAMON

¼ TEASPOON CAYENNE PEPPER

Upside-Down Cakes

I adore the combination of blueberries and cornmeal, and they are especially delicious together in this homey dessert. The blueberries and brown sugar at the bottom of each dish are more than a topping. They moisten and flavor the little cakes throughout, giving them a sticky fruit and toffee texture. Warm from the oven, they are delicious on their own and even better with a little scoop of vanilla ice cream on the side.

1. Preheat the oven to 375 degrees. Coat six 6-ounce ramekins with nonstick cooking spray.
2. Combine the brown sugar and ¼ cup (½ stick) of the butter in a small skillet and heat over medium-high heat, whisking, until the butter is melted and the sugar is dissolved. Divide among the ramekins, swirling to coat the bottoms, and set aside.
3. In a medium bowl, cream the remaining ¼ cup (½ stick) butter and the granulated sugar with an electric mixer until smooth. Add the eggs and beat until well incorporated. Stir in the milk, then stir in the flour, cornmeal, baking powder, and salt.
4. Divide the blueberries between the ramekins. Spoon the batter over them, smoothing it with a spatula. Bake until firm and golden, about 20 minutes.
5. Transfer the ramekins to a wire rack and run a sharp paring knife around the edge of each one. Place a small plate over each ramekin and use an oven mitt to invert, gently shaking to release the cake. Serve immediately.

Makes 6

NONSTICK COOKING SPRAY

6 TABLESPOONS FIRMLY PACKED LIGHT BROWN SUGAR

½ CUP (1 STICK) UNSALTED BUTTER, SOFTENED

¼ CUP GRANULATED SUGAR

2 LARGE EGGS

½ CUP WHOLE OR 2% MILK

¼ CUP UNBLEACHED ALL-PURPOSE FLOUR

¾ CUP YELLOW CORNMEAL

1 TEASPOON BAKING POWDER

¼ TEASPOON SALT

1 CUP FRESH BLUEBERRIES, PICKED OVER FOR STEMS

Mini Goat Cheese Cakes

WITH FRESH STRAWBERRIES

Cooling these cakes by setting the muffin tin in an ice bath as soon as they come out of the oven keeps them creamy and gets them on the table in 30 minutes. If you want to make them ahead of time, unmold them, drape with plastic wrap, and refrigerate for up to 6 hours before transferring to dessert plates and serving.

1. Preheat the oven to 350 degrees. Coat a 6-cup muffin tin with nonstick cooking spray.

2. In a large bowl, cream together the cream cheese, goat cheese, and 6 tablespoons of the sugar with an electric mixer until smooth. Add the whole egg, egg yolk, and vanilla and beat until well incorporated. Stir in the flour. Spoon the batter into the muffin tin cups and smooth the tops with a spatula.

3. Bake until the cakes are set around the edges but still a little jiggly in the center, about 15 minutes.

4. While the cakes are baking, fill a 9 x 11-inch baking pan with 1 inch of ice water and set it on a wire rack. Combine the strawberries and remaining 2 tablespoons sugar in a small bowl and let stand, stirring once or twice, to dissolve the sugar.

5. Remove the muffin tin from the oven, set it in ice water, and let stand until the cakes are cooled, 5 to 7 minutes.

6. Invert the muffin tin onto a platter, use a wide metal spatula to transfer each cake to a dessert plate, and serve immediately with the strawberries spooned over each.

Makes 6

NONSTICK COOKING SPRAY

TWO 3-OUNCE PACKAGES CREAM CHEESE, SOFTENED

4 OUNCES FRESH GOAT CHEESE

1/2 CUP GRANULATED SUGAR

1 LARGE EGG

1 LARGE EGG YOLK

1 TEASPOON VANILLA EXTRACT

1 1/2 TABLESPOONS UNBLEACHED ALL-PURPOSE FLOUR

3/4 CUP FRESH STRAWBERRIES, HULLED AND SLICED

LITTLE ALMOND

Tea Cakes

A large proportion of almond paste gives these cupcakes a moist and dense texture, perfect for nibbling with a cup of strong tea. They're delicate, so let them sit in the pan for 5 minutes to solidify before turning them out and eating warm.

1. Preheat the oven to 400 degrees. Grease a 6-cup muffin tin with butter.

2. In a large bowl, cream the ¼ cup butter and the granulated sugar with an electric mixer until smooth, scraping down the sides of the bowl once or twice as necessary. Add the almond paste, egg, and almond extract and beat, scraping down the bowl once, until well combined. Add the flour, baking powder, and salt and mix on low until just combined. Spoon the batter into the muffin tin cups and smooth the tops with a spatula. Sprinkle each with the almonds.

3. Bake until the tops of the cupcakes are just golden, 16 to 18 minutes. Remove the pan from the oven, set on a wire rack, and let sit for 5 minutes before inverting the pan to remove the tea cakes. Sift with confectioners' sugar just before serving.

Makes 6

¼ CUP (½ STICK) UNSALTED BUTTER, SOFTENED; PLUS MORE FOR GREASING THE PAN

6 TABLESPOONS GRANULATED SUGAR

¼ CUP (ABOUT 3 OUNCES) ALMOND PASTE

1 LARGE EGG

¼ TEASPOON ALMOND EXTRACT

3 TABLESPOONS UNBLEACHED ALL-PURPOSE FLOUR

¼ TEASPOON BAKING POWDER

¼ TEASPOON SALT

1½ TABLESPOONS SLICED BLANCHED ALMONDS

CONFECTIONERS' SUGAR

Baked Apple-Raspberry Pancake

This is a variation on a baked apple pancake recipe I've been making for years, with a sprinkling of raspberries added for color and tart flavor. Make it in the early fall, when both fruits are in season, or use frozen berries (I keep a bag on hand always for quick desserts and use them straight from the freezer) when good raspberries are unavailable. The batter comes together in a food processor in an instant, and the cake bakes quickly.

1. Preheat the oven to 450 degrees.
2. Melt 3 tablespoons of the butter in a 10-inch ovenproof skillet. Stir in the sliced apple and ¼ cup of the granulated sugar. Cook over medium heat, stirring once or twice, until the slices are a little bit softened and the sugar begins to caramelize, 3 to 4 minutes.
3. While the apples are cooking, melt the remaining 2 tablespoons butter in a small pan or in a small microwave-safe bowl in the microwave. Combine the melted butter, eggs, milk, the remaining ¼ cup granulated sugar, the vanilla, cinnamon, salt, and flour in a food processor and pulse several times.
4. Stir the raspberries into the skillet with the apples. Pour in the batter. Sprinkle with the brown sugar. Bake until puffed and golden, about 15 minutes. Slice and serve with vanilla ice cream on the side if desired.

Serves 6

5 TABLESPOONS UNSALTED BUTTER

1 MEDIUM GRANNY SMITH OR OTHER TART APPLE, PEELED, CORED, AND THINLY SLICED

½ CUP GRANULATED SUGAR

3 LARGE EGGS

¾ CUP WHOLE OR 2% MILK

½ TEASPOON VANILLA EXTRACT

¼ TEASPOON GROUND CINNAMON

¼ TEASPOON SALT

½ CUP UNBLEACHED ALL-PURPOSE FLOUR

½ CUP FRESH OR THAWED FROZEN RASPBERRIES

3 TABLESPOONS FIRMLY PACKED LIGHT BROWN SUGAR

VANILLA ICE CREAM (OPTIONAL)

Dessert Waffles

There's no quicker way to bake cake batter than in a waffle iron. I like the thickness and deep indentations of Belgian waffles, but the recipe will work in any type of waffle iron. These are sweet and delicious served hot from the press, with a dusting of powdered sugar.

1. Heat the waffle iron according to the manufacturer's instructions.

2. Whisk the flour, pecans, baking powder, salt, cinnamon, brown sugar, and granulated sugar in a large bowl. Whisk the melted butter, milk, sour cream, and eggs in a medium bowl. Stir the wet ingredients into the dry ingredients until moistened.

3. Coat the grids of the iron with nonstick cooking spray. Pour some of the batter (how much depends on the size of your waffle iron) onto the grids and spread it to the edges with a spatula. Cook until golden brown, 3 to 6 minutes, depending on your machine. Transfer to a plate and loosely tent with aluminum foil. Repeat with the remaining batter, coating the grids with more spray before beginning each new batch.

4. Dust the waffles with confectioners' sugar and serve immediately with sweetened whipped cream, if desired.

Makes 6

1½ CUPS UNBLEACHED ALL-PURPOSE FLOUR

½ CUP PECANS, FINELY CHOPPED

1 TABLESPOON BAKING POWDER

¼ TEASPOON SALT

¼ TEASPOON GROUND CINNAMON

¾ CUP FIRMLY PACKED LIGHT BROWN SUGAR

¼ CUP GRANULATED SUGAR

6 TABLESPOONS (¾ STICK) UNSALTED BUTTER, MELTED AND COOLED

1 CUP WHOLE OR 2% MILK

½ CUP SOUR CREAM (NOT LOW- OR REDUCED-FAT)

2 LARGE EGGS, LIGHTLY BEATEN

NONSTICK COOKING SPRAY

CONFECTIONERS' SUGAR

SWEETENED WHIPPED CREAM (OPTIONAL)

MILK CHOCOLATE BROWNIE WAFFLES AND ESPRESSO BROWNIE WAFFLES

Brownie Waffles

✳

These rich dessert waffles are a cross between cake and brownies. Serve them on their own, with whipped cream and berries, or topped with coffee ice cream and caramel sauce if you want to go over the top.

1. Heat the waffle iron according to the manufacturer's instructions.
2. Combine the chocolate and butter in a microwave-safe bowl. Melt the chocolate in the microwave on high for 1½ to 2 minutes, depending on the power and size of your microwave. Stir until smooth.
3. Whisk the brown sugar, eggs, vanilla, and milk in a large bowl. Whisk in the chocolate mixture. Sift the cocoa through a fine strainer into the bowl. Stir in the flour, baking powder, and salt.
4. Coat the grids of the iron with nonstick cooking spray. Pour some of the batter (how much depends on the size of your waffle iron) over the grids and spread it to the edges with a spatula. Cook until firm and baked through, 3 to 6 minutes, depending on your machine. Transfer to a plate and loosely tent with aluminum foil. Repeat with the remaining batter, coating the grids with more spray before beginning each new batch. Serve immediately.

Makes 6

6 OUNCES MILK CHOCOLATE, FINELY CHOPPED

½ CUP (1 STICK) UNSALTED BUTTER

1 CUP FIRMLY PACKED LIGHT BROWN SUGAR

4 LARGE EGGS

2 TEASPOONS VANILLA EXTRACT

½ CUP WHOLE OR 2% MILK

¼ CUP UNSWEETENED DUTCH-PROCESS COCOA POWDER

¾ CUP UNBLEACHED ALL-PURPOSE FLOUR

1 TEASPOON BAKING POWDER

¼ TEASPOON SALT

NONSTICK COOKING SPRAY

Espresso Brownie Waffles

A large amount of instant espresso powder gives these rich waffles a strong coffee edge.
Topped with coffee ice cream, they are a coffee lover's delight.

1. Heat the waffle iron according to the manufacturer's instructions.
2. Combine the butter and chocolate in a small microwave-safe bowl. Melt the chocolate in the microwave on high for 30 seconds to 1 minute, depending on the power and size of your microwave. Stir until smooth.
3. Whisk the eggs, sugar, espresso powder, and vanilla in a large bowl. Whisk in the chocolate mixture. Stir in the flour, baking powder, and salt.
4. Coat the grids of the iron with nonstick cooking spray. Pour some of the batter (how much depends on the size of your waffle iron) over the grids and spread it to the edges with a spatula. Cook until firm and baked through, 3 to 6 minutes, depending on your machine. Transfer to a plate and loosely tent with aluminum foil. Repeat with the remaining batter, coating the grids with more spray before beginning each new batch. Serve immediately, topped with coffee ice cream.

Makes 6

- ½ CUP (1 STICK) UNSALTED BUTTER, CUT INTO PIECES
- 3 OUNCES UNSWEETENED CHOCOLATE, CHOPPED
- 2 LARGE EGGS
- 1¼ CUPS GRANULATED SUGAR
- 3 TABLESPOONS INSTANT ESPRESSO POWDER
- 1 TEASPOON VANILLA EXTRACT
- ¾ CUP UNBLEACHED ALL-PURPOSE FLOUR
- ½ TEASPOON BAKING POWDER
- ¼ TEASPOON SALT
- NONSTICK COOKING SPRAY
- 1 PINT COFFEE ICE CREAM

Cheddar Waffles

WITH PEARS & HONEY

*This is a wonderful alternative to apple pie with Cheddar. I make these waffles
in the fall, with local cheese, pears, and honey from the farmers' market.*

1. Heat the waffle iron according to the manufacturer's instructions.
   Melt the butter in medium skillet and set aside to cool

2. Stir the flour, baking powder, salt, and sugar in a large bowl.

3. Measure the milk into a large glass measuring cup. Crack the
   egg into the cup and beat lightly with a fork to break it up. Stir
   in 4 tablespoons of the melted butter, leaving the remaining
   2 tablespoons in the skillet. Stir in the cheese.

4. Coat the grids of the iron with nonstick cooking spray. Pour some
   of the batter (how much depends on the size of your waffle iron)
   onto the grids and spread it to the edges with a spatula. Cook until
   golden brown, 3 to 6 minutes. Transfer to a plate and loosely tent
   with aluminum foil. Repeat with the remaining batter, coating the
   grids with more spray before beginning the new batch.

5. While the waffles are cooking, place the skillet with the remaining
   melted butter over medium heat and add the pears and honey.
   Cook, stirring frequently, until the pears are softened but still hold
   their shape and are beginning to brown, 5 to 7 minutes.

6. To serve, spoon some pears over each waffle and serve immediately
   with more honey for drizzling on the side.

Makes 4

6 TABLESPOONS (3/4 STICK)
UNSALTED BUTTER

1 1/2 CUPS UNBLEACHED ALL-
PURPOSE FLOUR

1 1/2 TEASPOONS BAKING POWDER

1/4 TEASPOON SALT

2 TABLESPOONS GRANULATED
SUGAR

1 1/2 CUPS WHOLE OR 2% MILK

1 LARGE EGG

1 CUP (ABOUT 2 OUNCES) GRATED
CHEDDAR

NONSTICK COOKING SPRAY

2 RIPE PEARS, PEELED, CORED,
AND SLICED

1/4 CUP HONEY; PLUS MORE FOR
DRIZZLING

Cinnamon-Scented Mini Bundt Cakes

WITH PEACHES & SOUR CREAM

*Small cakes bake much more quickly than a larger cake would. So when I want cake
in 30 minutes or so, I often pull out my mini Bundt tin (it's the same size as a 6-cup muffin
tin, which you can use instead) to create these quick little cakes. A garnish of sour cream,
sliced peaches, and a sprinkling of brown sugar is rustic but elegant and complements
the fragrant and meltingly tender cakes.*

1. Preheat the oven to 350 degrees. Coat a 6-cup mini Bundt cake pan with nonstick cooking spray.

2. In a large bowl, cream the butter and granulated sugar with an electric mixer until fluffy, about 3 minutes, scraping down the sides of the bowl once or twice as necessary. Add the eggs and vanilla and beat until smooth, again scraping down the bowl as necessary. Add the flour, baking powder, cinnamon, and salt and beat on low just until combined. When all of the flour has been incorporated, scrape down the bowl and beat for 1 minute. Spoon the batter into the Bundt cake cups and smooth the tops with a spatula.

3. Bake the cakes until golden, about 20 minutes. Put the pan on a wire rack and let cool 5 minutes. Invert and transfer each cake to a dessert plate. Mound some sour cream in the center of or alongside of each cake, top with the peaches, sprinkle with the brown sugar, and serve.

Serves 6

NONSTICK COOKING SPRAY

3/4 CUP (1 1/2 STICKS) UNSALTED BUTTER, SOFTENED

1 CUP PLUS 2 TABLESPOONS GRANULATED SUGAR

3 LARGE EGGS

1 1/2 TEASPOONS VANILLA EXTRACT

1 CUP PLUS 2 TABLESPOONS CAKE FLOUR

1/2 TEASPOON BAKING POWDER

1 TEASPOON GROUND CINNAMON

1/4 TEASPOON SALT

3/4 CUP SOUR CREAM (NOT LOW- OR REDUCED-FAT)

1/4 CUP FIRMLY PACKED LIGHT BROWN SUGAR

2 RIPE PEACHES, PITTED AND CUT INTO 8 WEDGES EACH

Lemon Soufflé Omelet

WITH VANILLA-SCENTED STRAWBERRIES

A more elegant relative of the puffed pancake, this old-fashioned dessert is shockingly
quick and easy to make. It won't rise as high as a traditional soufflé baked in a dish, but it
has the same melt-in-your-mouth texture with less work and worry.

1. Preheat the oven to 400 degrees.
2. Put the egg whites in a medium bowl and whip with an electric mixer on high until foamy. With the mixer running, add 6 tablespoons of the sugar in a slow, steady stream and continue to whip until the egg whites just hold stiff peaks.
3. In a large bowl, beat the yolks on high until thick and pale, about 5 minutes. Stir in the lemon juice and zest, and the flour. Using a rubber spatula, gently fold the egg whites into the egg yolk mixture, taking care not to deflate the whites.
4. Melt the butter in a 10-inch ovenproof skillet over low heat and swirl to coat the bottom of the pan. Scrape the soufflé mixture into the pan and smooth the top with the spatula. Bake until golden and puffed, 10 to 12 minutes.
5. While the soufflé is baking, hull and slice the strawberries, then combine them with the remaining 2 tablespoons sugar and the vanilla in a small bowl. Let stand for 5 minutes, stirring a few times to dissolve the sugar.
6. Remove the soufflé from the oven, spoon into dessert bowls, top with the strawberries, and serve immediately.

Serves 4

4 LARGE EGGS, SEPARATED

½ CUP GRANULATED SUGAR

3 TABLESPOONS FRESH LEMON JUICE

1 TEASPOON FINELY GRATED LEMON ZEST

1 TABLESPOON UNBLEACHED ALL-PURPOSE FLOUR

2 TABLESPOONS UNSALTED BUTTER

1 PINT FRESH STRAWBERRIES, RINSED AND PATTED DRY

½ TEASPOON VANILLA EXTRACT

Chapter 3

PRESTO *Pastry!*

Traditional pie and tart doughs take time: time to mix, time to chill, time to roll, and time to bake. What to do if you want a dessert that satisfies like pie, but have only a half hour to produce it? In this chapter, you'll find some deliciously creative answers to this question.

The simplest fix is as close as your bread box. Instead of making pastry dough from scratch, use bread as a base for your dessert. Split and toasted English muffins spread with mascarpone and cherry preserves make sweet little tarts. Slices of country bread provide the crust for individual broiled nectarine tarts with a lemon-poppy seed compound butter. Thick slices of baguette slit down the middle and stuffed with chocolate, nuts, and dried fruit make delicious dessert French toast. And dessert versions of the grilled cheese sandwich, filled with fruit and goat cheese or Nutella® and jam, are like buttery turnovers but without the fuss. If your taste in pastry tends toward the soft and yielding, use tortillas to make quick crepe-like desserts filled with bananas and dressed with chocolate sauce or stuffed with caramelized apples and oozing with whipped cream.

Dough from the freezer case is another option. Prepared pie crusts are always a disappointment, but frozen pizza dough is fabulous. So take a cue from Italian cooks and make dessert pizza. In Italy, pizza dough is sometimes topped with grapes, but I like to crown mine with thinly sliced apples for a distinctly American version. Phyllo dough, also found in the freezer case, is flaky and crisp like puff pastry, but bakes up much more quickly. Use it to make a minimalist fruit tart topped with sliced mango, or break it into pieces and layer with fruit and whipped cream to make rustic napoleons.

For quick pastry from scratch, you have a couple of choices. Put your pastry on top, rather than underneath your fruit: Fruit crisps and cobblers require less oven time than pies and tarts. Peaches sprinkled with a crunchy cornmeal-pine nut topping is unusual. Blueberries topped with cream cheese biscuit dough is comforting. Finally, baking powder biscuit dough is so easy to make and bakes to perfection in 12 minutes, enough time for you to whip cream and slice fruit for divine shortcakes. You just need 30 minutes, and it's much easier than pie.

Also in this chapter is absolutely the quickest way to produce a homemade fruit and pastry dessert: Dip apple slices in beer batter and deep-fry them. In the time it takes to heat the oil, you can make your batter. Two to three minutes in the pot is all it takes to get a tempura-like crust around each slice of apple. The slices are addictive, so don't be surprised if every one of them has been eaten before 30 minutes has elapsed.

Sour Cherry & Cheese Tarts

Toasted English muffins provide a base for these quick tarts, great for after a casual supper or as an indulgent breakfast. Look for best-quality preserves with plump whole cherries for the tastiest results. You can also use fresh fruit here—thinly sliced strawberries, peaches, or plums are great. Sprinkle the fruit with a little sugar before returning the tarts to the broiler to give them a sweet crust.

1. Combine the mascarpone and confectioners' sugar in a small bowl.
2. Preheat the broiler. Arrange the split English muffins on a baking sheet and toast under the broiler until lightly golden, 30 seconds to 1 minute.
3. Spread some mascarpone over each muffin half. Spoon 1 tablespoon of preserves on top of the mascarpone. Return to the broiler and toast until the cheese is bubbling and the edges of the muffins are well browned, another 30 seconds to 1 minute. Serve immediately.

Serves 4

1/2 CUP MASCARPONE

1 TABLESPOON CONFECTIONERS' SUGAR

2 ENGLISH MUFFINS, SPLIT IN HALF

1/4 CUP SOUR CHERRY PRESERVES

French Toast

In France, French toast is considered a dessert, not a breakfast. So why not do as the French do and take a few minutes to transform a few slices of leftover baguette into a sweet treat? All you'll need are a few pantry items and a skillet. Make sure you slice your bread thick enough, about 1½ inches, so you can create a large pocket for the filling.

1. Combine the chocolate chips, cranberries, and pecans in a small bowl.

2. Make a long pocket in each slice of bread by cutting into one side from end to end with a sharp paring knife to within ¼ inch of the opposite side. Pull open each pocket and stuff with some of the chocolate chip mixture. Pinch and squeeze the bread along the opening to enclose the filling.

3. Beat the eggs and heavy cream with a fork in a pie plate or shallow bowl. Put the stuffed bread slices in the plate and let stand, turning once with tongs, until the bread absorbs the egg mixture, about 5 minutes.

4. Melt the butter in a large skillet over medium-low heat. Put the soaked bread slices in the skillet and cook until golden on both sides, turning once, 8 to 10 minutes total.

5. Transfer each slice to a dessert plate, dust heavily with confectioners' sugar, and serve immediately.

Makes 4

¼ CUP MINI SEMISWEET CHOCOLATE CHIPS

2 TABLESPOONS SWEETENED DRIED CRANBERRIES

2 TABLESPOONS FINELY CHOPPED PECANS

FOUR 1½-INCH-THICK, 6-INCH-LONG DIAGONAL BAGUETTE SLICES

2 LARGE EGGS

¾ CUP HEAVY CREAM

2 TABLESPOONS UNSALTED BUTTER

CONFECTIONERS' SUGAR FOR DUSTING

Sandwiches

This has to be one of my favorite dessert discoveries, goat cheese and nectarines
sandwiched between two slices of bread and grilled in butter until golden.
Cut into large triangles, the finished sandwiches are like warm cheese turnovers,
bursting with sweet and tart flavor.

1. Spread the jam on two of the slices of bread. Spread the goat cheese on the two remaining slices.
2. Melt 1 tablespoon of the butter in a large skillet over medium-low heat. Add the nectarine wedges and granulated sugar and cook, turning a few times, until the wedges are soft but not falling apart, 3 to 5 minutes. Remove the pan from the heat and arrange the wedges on top of the goat cheese–covered bread. Top with the jam-covered bread, pressing lightly so the goat cheese adheres to the nectarines.
3. Melt the remaining 1 tablespoon butter in the skillet over medium heat and cook the sandwiches, turning once, until golden on both sides, 5 to 7 minutes total. Cut each sandwich diagonally into two triangles, dust with confectioners' sugar, and serve immediately.

Makes 2, serves 4

1 TABLESPOON STRAWBERRY OR RASPBERRY JAM

4 SLICES FIRM WHITE BREAD

2 OUNCES SOFT GOAT CHEESE

2 TABLESPOONS UNSALTED BUTTER

1 NECTARINE, PITTED AND CUT INTO 10 WEDGES

1 TABLESPOON GRANULATED SUGAR

CONFECTIONERS' SUGAR FOR DUSTING

Nectarine Tartlets

WITH LEMON-POPPY SEED BUTTER

I love to use nectarines in tarts. They're sweet like peaches, but with a nice, smooth skin that doesn't need to be peeled. Here, I arrange sliced fruit on top of bread and dot it with butter that's been blended with honey, lemon zest, and poppy seeds. It's a great way to add richness and flavor to this rustic dessert without a lot of work.

1. Preheat the oven to 400 degrees.
2. Put the honey, butter, poppy seeds, lemon zest, and vanilla in a small bowl. Mash with the back of a spoon until well combined.
3. Arrange the bread slices on a baking sheet and toast in the oven until just crisp, about 5 minutes.
4. Preheat the broiler. Arrange the nectarines on top of the toasted bread slices. Dot with the honey-butter mixture. Broil until the fruit is warmed through and softened, 5 to 7 minutes. Remove from the oven and serve immediately.

Makes 4

3 TABLESPOONS HONEY

3 TABLESPOONS UNSALTED BUTTER, SOFTENED

1 TEASPOON POPPY SEEDS

½ TEASPOON GRATED LEMON ZEST

¼ TEASPOON VANILLA EXTRACT

FOUR ½-INCH-THICK SLICES COUNTRY BREAD

2 NECTARINES, PITTED AND EACH CUT INTO 8 WEDGES

Banana & Walnut Quesadillas

WITH QUICK CHOCOLATE SAUCE

Flour tortillas become a delicious pastry container for warmed bananas in this simple dessert inspired by the quesadilla. Don't skip the chocolate sauce. It couldn't be simpler— just pour hot cream over chopped chocolate, let stand while you prepare the quesadillas, and whisk until smooth before drizzling over the warm wedges.

1. Put the chocolate in a heatproof bowl. Bring the heavy cream to boil in a small, heavy saucepan and pour over the chocolate. Let stand for 5 minutes, then whisk until smooth. Set aside.

2. Melt 1 tablespoon of the butter over medium-low heat in a large skillet and stir in 1 tablespoon of the sugar. Put one tortilla in the skillet. Arrange half of the sliced bananas in a single layer on one side of the tortilla. Sprinkle with 2 tablespoons of the walnuts and another 2 tablespoons of the sugar. Cook until the bottom of the tortilla is light golden. Fold the other side of the tortilla over the bananas and cook until the bananas are heated through, another 2 to 3 minutes. Slide the quesadilla onto a plate, wipe out the skillet with a paper towel, and repeat with the remaining ingredients.

3. Slice each quesadilla into 4 wedges, drizzle with chocolate sauce, and serve immediately.

Makes 2

2 OUNCES BITTERSWEET CHOCOLATE, FINELY CHOPPED

6 TABLESPOONS HEAVY CREAM

2 TABLESPOONS UNSALTED BUTTER

6 TABLESPOONS GRANULATED SUGAR

TWO 9- OR 10-INCH FLOUR TORTILLAS

2 SMALL RIPE BANANAS, PEELED AND CUT INTO 1/4-INCH-THICK ROUNDS

1/4 CUP FINELY CHOPPED WALNUTS

Apple Tortilla Crepes

Tortillas are sturdier than crepes, the better to hold this chunky filling of caramelized apples. Soften and enrich them by brushing with melted butter and keeping them warm in the oven while you cook the apples. A rustic but also elegant dessert, these crepes are great for brunch, drizzled with maple syrup in place of the cinnamon sugar.

1. Preheat the oven to 200 degrees.
2. Combine ¼ teaspoon of the cinnamon and 2 tablespoons of the sugar in a small bowl.
3. Melt the butter over medium heat in a large skillet. Brush each tortilla with a little bit of the melted butter, stack the buttered tortillas on a plate, loosely cover with aluminum foil, and keep warm in the oven.
4. Add the apples, the remaining ¼ teaspoon cinnamon, the ginger, and 4 tablespoons of the sugar to the pan and cook, stirring often, until the apples are softened and caramelized, 5 to 7 minutes.
5. Combine the heavy cream, sour cream, and remaining 1 tablespoon sugar in a medium bowl and whip with an electric mixer on medium-high speed until the cream just holds stiff peaks.
6. Remove the tortillas from the oven and place each one on a dessert plate. Spoon the apples onto one side of each tortilla. Spoon the whipped cream over the apples, fold the tortilla over, and serve immediately.

Makes 4

½ TEASPOON GROUND CINNAMON

7 TABLESPOONS GRANULATED SUGAR

¼ CUP (½ STICK) UNSALTED BUTTER

FOUR 9- OR 10-INCH FLOUR TORTILLAS

4 SMALL GRANNY SMITH APPLES, PEELED, CORED, AND CUT INTO ½-INCH CHUNKS

¼ TEASPOON GROUND GINGER

½ CUP HEAVY CREAM

2 TABLESPOONS SOUR CREAM (NOT LOW- OR REDUCED-FAT)

Panini

Nutella, the hazelnut-and-chocolate spread so popular in Europe, makes a delicious filling for French toast. If you'd like, leave out the raspberries and use a different flavor of jam to vary the recipes—orange marmalade is great, and so are fig preserves.

1. Spread two slices of the bread with the jam and arrange the raspberries on top, pressing down on them lightly so they adhere. Spread the other two slices of bread with the Nutella and place them, Nutella side down, on top of the raspberries.

2. Whisk the eggs, cream, confectioners' sugar, and vanilla in a pie plate or shallow bowl. Put one of the sandwiches in the mixture and turn to completely coat it. Transfer to a platter. Repeat with the remaining sandwich. Let stand on the platter for a few minutes to absorb the egg.

3. Melt the butter in a large skillet over medium heat, then cook the sandwiches, turning once, until golden on both sides, 5 to 7 minutes total. Cut each sandwich diagonally into 2 triangles, dust with confectioners' sugar, and serve immediately.

Makes 2; serves 4

4 SLICES BRIOCHE OR BEST-QUALITY WHITE BREAD

2 TABLESPOONS RASPBERRY JAM

10 FRESH RASPBERRIES

1/4 CUP NUTELLA

2 LARGE EGGS

1/4 CUP HEAVY CREAM

2 TABLESPOONS CONFECTIONERS' SUGAR; PLUS MORE FOR DUSTING

1 TEASPOON VANILLA EXTRACT

2 TABLESPOONS UNSALTED BUTTER

Apple Pizza

Sweet pizzas are a long-standing tradition in Italy, so why not enjoy them here? Frozen pizza dough is rather soft and delicate, well-suited to take the place of pie crust. Thinly slicing the apples and baking the dough in a very hot oven make this dessert a quick fix.

1. Preheat the oven to 500 degrees. Grease the bottom of a 16 x 11-inch rimmed baking sheet with butter.

2. Combine the sugar and cinnamon in a small bowl.

3. Press and stretch the dough evenly into a rough 11-inch round on the prepared baking sheet, then fold the edge inward ½ inch to create a lip. (If the dough resists at first, let it rest for a minute and then continue.) Arrange the apples in rows on top of the pizza, overlapping them. Sprinkle all over with the cinnamon sugar. Dot the apples with the bits of butter.

4. Bake the pizza until the underside of the dough is golden (you can lift up the pizza with a metal spatula and take a peek) and the apples are soft, about 15 minutes. Cut into 6 wedges and serve warm.

Makes one 11-inch pizza; serves 6

BUTTER FOR GREASING THE PAN

⅓ CUP GRANULATED SUGAR

½ TEASPOON GROUND CINNAMON

1 POUND FROZEN PIZZA DOUGH, THAWED

3 LARGE GRANNY SMITH APPLES, PEELED, CORED, AND CUT INTO ⅛-INCH-THICK SLICES

2 TABLESPOONS UNSALTED BUTTER, CUT INTO BITS

Apricot-Ricotta Tarts

All of the elements of a great fruit tart are here: juicy fruit, creamy filling, crisp crust. They're just put together out of order and at the last minute. If you've never worked with phyllo before it's really simple. Brush melted butter on a sheet, sprinkle with sugar and nuts, add another sheet, and repeat until you have four layers. Then bake until caramelized and crisp. Keep the stack of phyllo covered with a damp paper towel as you work, or it will dry out, and wrap the leftover dough tightly in plastic and refrigerate until you're ready to use it again.

1. Preheat the oven to 425 degrees. Line a baking sheet with parchment.
2. Combine the sugar and walnuts in a small bowl.
3. Lay one sheet of phyllo on the baking sheet and brush it with one third of the melted butter. Sprinkle with one third of the sugar-and-nut mixture. Repeat the layering two more times. Lay the last sheet of phyllo on top. Bake the phyllo until dark golden, 6 to 8 minutes. Slide the parchment and phyllo onto a wire rack, and let cool completely, about 10 minutes.
4. Meanwhile, combine the ricotta, 2 tablespoons of the honey, and the mint in a large measuring cup. Divide the ricotta between 4 dessert plates. Arrange a quartered apricot on top of each mound. Drizzle each apricot with some of the remaining 2 table-spoons honey. Break the baked phyllo sheets into shards and arrange on top of and around the apricots, reserving leftovers for another use. Serve immediately.

Serves 4

¾ CUP GRANULATED SUGAR

⅓ CUP FINELY CHOPPED WALNUTS

4 SHEETS FROZEN PHYLLO DOUGH, THAWED

6 TABLESPOONS (¾ STICK) UNSALTED BUTTER, MELTED AND SLIGHTLY COOLED

1½ CUPS WHOLE-MILK RICOTTA CHEESE

¼ CUP HONEY

2 TABLESPOONS FINELY CHOPPED FRESH MINT

4 FRESH APRICOTS, PITTED AND QUARTERED

Peachy Pine Nut Crisp

Pre-peeled and sliced frozen fruit is a wonderful timesaver under certain circumstances. I use it in the winter, when local fruit isn't available. In desserts like this, where the fruit is peeled, sliced, and baked until very soft, it is every bit as good as produce shipped in from Florida, California, or South America. (Of course, you can use an equivalent amount of fresh fruit—you'll just need a few extra minutes of prep time for peeling, pitting, and slicing.) Pine nuts added to cornmeal give the crisp a rustic Italian flavor. This recipe is endlessly adaptable—try almonds, pecans, walnuts, or even pistachios in the topping and substitute apples, pears, or plums for the peaches.

1. Preheat the oven to 450 degrees.
2. Combine the peaches, granulated sugar, cornstarch, and vanilla in a large bowl and let stand, stirring once or twice, until the sugar is dissolved, about 5 minutes.
3. Combine the flour, cornmeal, brown sugar, nutmeg, and pine nuts in a medium bowl. Add the butter and mix on low speed with an electric mixer just until clumps begin to form, 1 to 2 minutes.
4. Spread the peaches across the bottom of an 8-inch-square baking pan. Sprinkle the topping evenly over the pears. Bake until the fruit is bubbling and the topping is golden, about 20 minutes. Serve warm.

Serves 6

4 CUPS FROZEN UNSWEETENED SLICED PEACHES (NO NEED TO THAW)

⅓ CUP GRANULATED SUGAR

1 TABLESPOON CORNSTARCH

½ TEASPOON VANILLA EXTRACT

6 TABLESPOONS UNBLEACHED ALL-PURPOSE FLOUR

⅓ CUP YELLOW CORNMEAL

¼ CUP FIRMLY PACKED LIGHT BROWN SUGAR

PINCH OF GROUND NUTMEG

¼ CUP PINE NUTS

¼ CUP (½ STICK) UNSALTED BUTTER, CHILLED AND CUT INTO SMALL PIECES

Biscuit Cobbler

All it takes is 15 minutes in a 450-degree oven to finish this terrific cobbler,
made by topping a pie plate full of blueberries with baking powder biscuit dough.
Cream cheese gives the biscuits unbelievable tenderness, while a little cornmeal gives
them flavor, color, and crunch. Serve warm, with or without vanilla ice cream.

1. Preheat the oven to 450 degrees. Butter an 8-inch glass pie plate.
2. Combine the blueberries, 3 tablespoons of the sugar, the lemon zest and juice, and cornstarch in a medium bowl, mashing some but not all of the blueberries with the back of a spoon, and let stand, stirring once or twice, until the sugar dissolves, about 5 minutes. Scrape the blueberries into the prepared pie plate.
3. Combine the flour, cornmeal, baking powder, salt, butter, and cream cheese in a food processor and pulse several times until the mixture resembles coarse meal. With the motor running, add the milk and process until a rough dough forms. Drop tablespoonfuls of the biscuit dough on top of the berries.
4. Bake until the fruit is bubbling and the biscuits are risen and golden, about 15 minutes. Let stand for 5 minutes and serve warm.

Serves 4

BUTTER FOR GREASING THE PIE PLATE

3 CUPS FRESH BLUEBERRIES, PICKED OVER FOR STEMS

6 TABLESPOONS GRANULATED SUGAR

1/2 TEASPOON GRATED LEMON ZEST

1 TABLESPOON FRESH LEMON JUICE

1 1/2 TEASPOONS CORNSTARCH

6 TABLESPOONS UNBLEACHED ALL-PURPOSE FLOUR

1/4 CUP YELLOW CORNMEAL

3/4 TEASPOON BAKING POWDER

1/8 TEASPOON SALT

1 1/2 TABLESPOONS UNSALTED BUTTER, CHILLED AND CUT INTO PIECES

2 TABLESPOONS CREAM CHEESE (DON'T USE NONFAT OR LOW-FAT), CHILLED AND CUT INTO PIECES

1/4 CUP WHOLE OR 2% MILK

Beer-Battered Apples

For one of the quickest and most satisfying pastry fixes, dip apple slices in a tempura-style batter and deep-fry them for a couple of minutes. Watch the apples carefully and adjust the heat as you fry them, lowering the temperature if you see later batches begin to darken too quickly. Although their aroma will tempt you to eat them straight from the pot, give them a minute or two to cool to a safe eating temperature.

1. Heat 2 inches of vegetable oil over medium-high heat in a large saucepan. Line a baking sheet with paper towels.
2. Whisk the flour, granulated sugar, cinnamon, salt, and beer in a medium bowl.
3. Put 8 of the apple slices in the bowl and toss to coat with the batter. Lift them with a slotted spoon, one at a time, from the bowl, letting any excess batter drip back into the bowl, and put them in the hot oil. (Test the oil by dipping a corner of an apple into it—it should bubble up; if it doesn't, let it heat some more.) Fry the slices, turning them once, until golden brown on both sides, 2 to 3 minutes total. Use a slotted spoon to transfer the fried slices to the baking sheet to drain. Repeat with the remaining slices. Let the fried apple slices rest for a minute or two and then dust the fried apple slices heavily with confectioners' sugar and serve immediately.

Makes 16 slices; serves 4

VEGETABLE OIL FOR FRYING

1/2 CUP UNBLEACHED ALL-PURPOSE FLOUR

2 TABLESPOONS GRANULATED SUGAR

1/4 TEASPOON GROUND CINNAMON

PINCH OF SALT

1/2 CUP LAGER-STYLE BEER, CHILLED

1 LARGE APPLE, PEELED, CORED, AND CUT INTO SIXTEEN 1/4-INCH-THICK SLICES

CONFECTIONERS' SUGAR FOR DUSTING

Phyllo Napoleons

Here, baked phyllo dough becomes a rustic napoleon-like dessert when layered with maple syrup–sweetened blueberries and cream. As with the recipe on page 72, you'll have extra phyllo. Break it up and snack on the crunchy pieces, or use it in a fruit dessert of your own devising.

1. Preheat the oven to 425 degrees. Line a baking sheet with parchment.
2. Combine the sugar and walnuts in a small bowl.
3. Lay one sheet of phyllo on the prepared baking sheet and brush with one third of the melted butter. Sprinkle with one third of the sugar-and-nut mixture. Repeat the layering two more times. Lay the last sheet of phyllo on top.
4. Bake the phyllo until dark golden, 6 to 8 minutes. Remove from the oven, slide the parchment onto a wire rack, and let cool completely, about 10 minutes.
5. Meanwhile, combine the maple syrup and blueberries in a small, heavy saucepan and bring to a boil. Reduce the heat to low and simmer for 5 minutes. Scrape into a bowl and let cool slightly, about 10 minutes.
6. Break the baked phyllo into rough squares about 4 inches square, reserving the leftovers for another use. Place a square on each of 4 dessert plates. Spoon the sour cream on top of each phyllo square. Spoon the blueberries over the sour cream. Top with another phyllo square. Serve immediately.

Serves 4

³/₄ CUP GRANULATED SUGAR

¹/₃ CUP FINELY CHOPPED WALNUTS

4 SHEETS FROZEN PHYLLO DOUGH, THAWED

6 TABLESPOONS (³/₄ STICK) UNSALTED BUTTER, MELTED AND SLIGHTLY COOLED

¹/₄ CUP PURE MAPLE SYRUP

1 PINT FRESH BLUEBERRIES, PICKED OVER FOR STEMS

1 CUP SOUR CREAM (NOT LOW-OR REDUCED-FAT)

Strawberry Shortcakes

Baking powder biscuits rise to lofty heights after just 10 minutes or so in a 500-degree oven. Minutes after they're baked, they can be split and filled with fruit and cream.

1. Preheat the oven to 500 degrees. Coat a baking sheet with nonstick cooking spray or line with parchment.

2. Cut the butter into ¼-inch dice and put in a small bowl in the freezer while you gather the rest of the ingredients.

3. Combine the flour, baking powder, brown sugar, and salt in a large bowl. Add the chilled butter pieces and, with an electric mixer on low, mix just until the mixture resembles coarse meal. Stir in ¾ cup plus 2 tablespoons of the heavy cream and mix on low just until a rough dough forms. Drop the dough in 6 mounds, at least 3 inches apart, onto the baking sheet. Bake until golden, about 12 minutes. Transfer the biscuits to a wire rack and let cool for 10 minutes.

4. While the biscuits are baking, combine the strawberries and ¼ cup of the granulated sugar in a medium bowl and let stand, stirring once or twice, to dissolve the sugar.

5. Whip the remaining 1 cup heavy cream and 2 tablespoons granulated sugar in a medium bowl with an electric mixer on medium-high speed until the cream just holds stiff peaks.

6. Split each biscuit in half and place the bottoms on 6 dessert plates. Spoon the macerated strawberries over the biscuit bottoms, top with a dollop of whipped cream, and then with the biscuit tops. Serve immediately.

Serves 6

NONSTICK COOKING SPRAY, IF NEEDED

6 TABLESPOONS (¾ STICK) UNSALTED BUTTER, CHILLED

2 CUPS UNBLEACHED ALL-PURPOSE FLOUR

1 TABLESPOON BAKING POWDER

¼ CUP FIRMLY PACKED LIGHT BROWN SUGAR

½ TEASPOON SALT

1¾ CUPS PLUS 2 TABLESPOONS HEAVY CREAM

1½ PINTS FRESH STRAWBERRIES, HULLED AND SLICED

6 TABLESPOONS GRANULATED SUGAR

SHORTCAKE VARIATIONS

Here are a few ways to vary the biscuit recipe (at left), with suggestions for fruit to match:

Cinnamon Shortcakes Add ½ teaspoon ground cinnamon to the flour mixture. Use sliced peaches instead of strawberries.

Lemon-Ginger Shortcakes Add 2 tablespoons finely chopped crystallized ginger, ½ teaspoon ground ginger, and 1 teaspoon grated lemon zest to the flour mixture. Use blueberries instead of strawberries

Oatmeal Shortcakes Add ½ cup old-fashioned rolled oats to the flour mixture, and 1 or 2 tablespoons of extra cream if necessary. Use sliced plums instead of strawberries.

Cornmeal Shortcakes Substitute ½ cup yellow cornmeal for ½ cup of the flour. Use sliced apricots instead of strawberries.

Cocoa Shortcakes Substitute 6 tablespoons Dutch-process unsweetened cocoa powder for 6 tablespoons of the flour. Use raspberries instead of strawberries.

Chapter 4

Hasty Puddings

CLEVER FOOLS

Dessert doesn't get much simpler than pudding. Put some ingredients in a pot, give them a stir while they cook, and spoon the comforting result into bowls, often in well under 30 minutes.

Chocolate, vanilla, and butterscotch puddings are made by thickening sweetened milk or cream with cornstarch and sometimes eggs. The fun is in giving these classics a little edge. I add interest to chocolate pudding by using bittersweet chocolate and adding a touch of mint. Vanilla pudding graduates from the nursery when flavored with bourbon-soaked raisins. A sprinkling of sea salt over portions of butterscotch pudding updates an old favorite and gives it surprising complexity.

Puddings made with rice and couscous have a little more texture. Cooked with coconut milk and chocolate, creamy grains of rice keep their shape but take on those flavors. For entirely different desserts, use espresso powder and anisette or lemon zest and poppy seeds to flavor your rice. Instant couscous takes less than 10 minutes to become a rich and creamy dessert pudding, so it's a good thing that you can plump up some prunes with brandy in less time by heating them in the microwave and letting them steep as your couscous cooks.

To enrich tapioca, I like to stir in some crème fraîche or white chocolate, both of which will give the pudding body and flavor. Tapioca can also be served warm, but I prefer it chilled and served with fruit or a fruit sauce. Setting the pudding over a bowl of ice and water cools and thickens the pudding in minutes. (I often turn to ice baths when I want to quickly cool all kinds of desserts. There's no reason you can't use one to cool rice pudding or couscous if you prefer it chilled.)

In general, bread puddings baked in the oven need over an hour to cook through. But if you assemble small portions in shallow crème brûlée dishes you can cut that time considerably. I like to make these individual bread puddings with day-old croissants, which require only a small amount of custard to transform into a light and airy puddings. Mini chocolate chips sprinkled between the layers of bread melt into a moist and delicious filling.

I end the chapter with some quick ideas for mousses and fruit fools to suit many tastes and occasions. A satisfying and simple mocha mousse is stabilized with marshmallows, eliminating the need for raw egg whites, which can be tricky to whip and pose a small but serious health risk. A mascarpone mousse, garnished with Savoiardi cookies and strawberries in balsamic vinegar, combines several wonderfully compatible flavors if Italy. Finally, I'll show you how to make two fruit fools, one with fresh berries and the other with tropical fruit purée from the freezer case. These last two recipes, no more than fruit folded together with whipped cream, represent dessert at its minimalist best.

Dark Chocolate Pudding

I like this recipe because almost all of the ingredients go right into the pot at the outset. Then you simply cook while whisking until it's done. Chocolate and mint are a classic combination, but one that can be bitter or harsh. I like to add a couple of egg yolks, some butter, and vanilla to smooth out the edges.

1. Combine the cornstarch, sugar, and salt in a medium-size, heavy saucepan. Add the chocolate, then whisk in the half-and-half and egg yolks. Bring to a boil over medium heat, whisking constantly, and continue to boil and whisk until thickened, 2 to 3 minutes.

2. Remove the pan from the heat and whisk in the butter and extracts until the butter is melted and incorporated. Spoon into dessert bowls and serve immediately, or scrape into a bowl, cover the surface with plastic wrap (this will keep a skin from forming), and refrigerate for up to 1 day before serving.

Serves 4

¼ CUP CORNSTARCH

6 TABLESPOONS GRANULATED SUGAR

PINCH OF SALT

8 OUNCES BITTERSWEET CHOCOLATE, FINELY CHOPPED

2½ CUPS HALF-AND-HALF

2 LARGE EGG YOLKS

2 TABLESPOONS UNSALTED BUTTER

½ TEASPOON VANILLA EXTRACT

½ TEASPOON PEPPERMINT EXTRACT

Milk Chocolate Pudding

*Dark chocolate is for sophisticates, but milk chocolate is beloved by everyone.
A little bit of unsweetened cocoa powder prevents this deliciously sweet pudding from
becoming cloying. Served warm from the pot, there's nothing more pleasurable and
comforting. Or, you can spoon it into ceramic bowls or goblets, cover with plastic wrap,
and refrigerate for up to 2 days and serve chilled.*

1. Combine the cornstarch, sugar, and cocoa in a medium-size, heavy saucepan. Whisk in ½ cup of the heavy cream until the mixture is smooth. Stir in the remaining ½ cup cream and the milk. Bring to a boil over medium heat, whisking constantly, and continue to boil and whisk until the mixture thickens, 2 to 3 minutes.

2. Remove from the heat and whisk in the chocolate until melted. Whisk in the vanilla. Scrape into heatproof ceramic bowls and serve.

Serves 4

3 TABLESPOONS CORNSTARCH

3 TABLESPOONS GRANULATED SUGAR

2 TABLESPOONS UNSWEETENED COCOA POWDER

1 CUP HEAVY CREAM

1 CUP WHOLE OR 2% MILK

4 OUNCES BEST-QUALITY MILK CHOCOLATE, FINELY CHOPPED

1 TEASPOON VANILLA EXTRACT

Vanilla Pudding

WITH BOURBON & GOLDEN RAISINS

Bourbon cuts the richness of this vanilla pudding and gives it a little edge.
Serve it warm, or cool it quickly by setting it over a bowl of ice.

1. If serving the pudding cold, fill a large bowl with ice and a little bit of water. Have a medium bowl that will fit inside the larger bowl at the ready. Put the bourbon and raisins in a small microwave-safe bowl, cover with plastic wrap, and microwave on high for 1 minute. Set aside to cool.

2. Whisk the sugar, cornstarch, salt, egg yolks, and ¼ cup of the half-and-half in a medium-size, heavy saucepan until smooth. Whisk in the remaining 2¼ cups half-and-half. Bring to a bare simmer over medium-low heat, whisking constantly. Reduce the heat to low and continue to cook, whisking, until the mixture thickens, about 1 minute.

3. Pour the pudding through a fine strainer into the smaller bowl. Stir in the vanilla and plumped raisins, with any of the remaining bourbon. Serve warm, or cover the surface of the pudding with plastic wrap (this will keep a skin from forming) and set the bowl on top of the ice bath. Let stand until the pudding is thickened and cooled, about 10 minutes. Remove the plastic wrap, whisk, and spoon into 4 dessert goblets. Serve immediately.

Serves 4

¼ CUP BOURBON

⅓ CUP GOLDEN RAISINS

⅔ CUP GRANULATED SUGAR

¼ CUP CORNSTARCH

¼ TEASPOON SALT

2 LARGE EGG YOLKS

2½ CUPS HALF-AND-HALF

1 TEASPOON VANILLA EXTRACT

Mocha Marshmallow Mousse

Here's a great way to make a light and fluffy chocolate mousse without whipping egg whites. Marshmallows—which are, after all, a type of meringue—give the mousse structure. I add a little espresso powder for depth and balance. Serve it to grown-ups and see if they can guess the secret ingredient.

1. Combine the milk, marshmallows, chocolate, and espresso powder in a medium-size, heavy saucepan and heat over low heat, whisking constantly, until the marshmallows and chocolate are melted and incorporated. Set the saucepan in a bowl of ice water and let stand, whisking often, until cool and thick, 15 to 20 minutes.

2. Meanwhile, combine the heavy cream and vanilla in a medium bowl and whip with an electric mixer on high until the cream just holds stiff peaks. Fold the cooled chocolate mixture into the whipped cream, leaving some streaks. Spoon into dessert goblets and serve immediately, or cover with plastic wrap and refrigerate for up to 1 day before serving.

Serves 4

3/4 CUP WHOLE OR 2% MILK

4 CUPS MINI MARSHMALLOWS

3 OUNCES BITTERSWEET CHOCOLATE, FINELY CHOPPED

2 TEASPOONS INSTANT ESPRESSO POWDER

3/4 CUP COLD HEAVY CREAM

1 TEASPOON VANILLA EXTRACT

Rice Pudding

This delicious pudding, served warm from the pot, is a combination of the comforting and the exotic.

1. Combine the rice, coconut milk, milk, and salt in a large, heavy saucepan and bring to a boil. Reduce the heat to medium low and simmer, stirring occasionally, until the rice is cooked through and tender, about 20 minutes.
2. Remove from the heat and stir in the sugar, chocolate, and vanilla until the sugar is dissolved and the chocolate is melted. Spoon into ceramic dessert bowls and serve warm, or cover the surface of the pudding with plastic wrap (this will keep a skin from forming), refrigerate for up to 1 day, and serve cold.

Serves 6

¾ CUP ARBORIO RICE

ONE 14-OUNCE CAN UNSWEETENED COCONUT MILK

1 CUP WHOLE OR 2% MILK

¼ TEASPOON SALT

½ CUP GRANULATED SUGAR

3 OUNCES BITTERSWEET CHOCOLATE, FINELY CHOPPED

1 TEASPOON VANILLA EXTRACT

Rice Pudding

Coffee and anise liqueur are a classic after-dinner combination, and they lend their sophisticated flavors to this simple rice pudding. Serve in demitasse cups, if you like, with chocolate-covered espresso beans on the side.

1. Combine the rice, milk, heavy cream, espresso powder, and salt in a large, heavy saucepan and bring to a boil. Reduce the heat to medium low and simmer, stirring occasionally, until the rice is cooked through and tender, about 20 minutes.
2. Remove from the heat and stir in the sugar until dissolved. Stir in the Sambuca. Spoon into ceramic dessert bowls and serve warm, or cover the surface of the pudding with plastic wrap (this will keep a skin from forming), refrigerate for up to 1 day, and serve cold.

Serves 6

¾ CUP ARBORIO RICE

2½ CUPS WHOLE OR 2% MILK

1 CUP HEAVY CREAM

1½ TABLESPOONS INSTANT ESPRESSO POWDER

¼ TEASPOON SALT

½ CUP GRANULATED SUGAR

1 TABLESPOON SAMBUCA OR OTHER ANISE-FLAVORED LIQUEUR

Rice Pudding

This delicious rice pudding, enriched at the end with egg yolks and cream, gets some crunch from a spoonful of poppy seeds. Serve it warm on its own in the winter, or chill it and top with sliced fruit or berries in the summer months.

1. Combine the rice, milk, sugar, lemon zest, and salt in a large, heavy saucepan and bring to a boil. Reduce the heat to medium low and simmer, stirring occasionally, until the rice is cooked through and tender, about 20 minutes.
2. Whisk the egg yolks and heavy cream in small bowl. Slowly whisk about ½ cup of the hot rice pudding into the egg yolk mixture, a few tablespoons at a time. Whisk the egg yolk mixture into the hot rice pudding. Return to the heat and cook, stirring, until the mixture just comes to a bare simmer. Remove from the heat and stir in the vanilla and poppy seeds.
3. Spoon the pudding into bowls and serve warm, or transfer to a large bowl, cover the surface of the pudding with plastic wrap (this will keep a skin from forming), and refrigerate for up to 3 days before serving.

Serves 6

¾ CUP ARBORIO RICE

3 CUPS WHOLE OR 2% MILK

½ CUP GRANULATED SUGAR

2 TEASPOONS FINELY GRATED LEMON ZEST

¼ TEASPOON SALT

2 LARGE EGG YOLKS

½ CUP HEAVY CREAM

1 TEASPOON VANILLA EXTRACT

2 TEASPOONS POPPY SEEDS

Warm Butterscotch Pudding

WITH SEA SALT

*Sea salt enhances the burnt caramel flavor in this simple butterscotch pudding.
I especially like the large and delicate flakes of Malden sea salt, imported from England,
which also adds a little crunch to the dessert.*

1. Whisk the egg yolks, cornstarch, and ½ cup of the milk in a small bowl and set aside.
2. Combine the butter and brown sugar in a medium-size, heavy saucepan. Cook over low heat, whisking, until the butter is melted and the sugar is dissolved. Add the remaining ½ cup milk and the heavy cream and whisk to combine. Whisk in the egg yolk mixture. Bring to a simmer and continue to cook, whisking constantly, until the mixture thickens, 3 to 4 minutes.
3. Scrape the pudding into heatproof ceramic bowls, sprinkle each portion with ¼ teaspoon of the sea salt, and serve immediately.

Serves 4

2 LARGE EGG YOLKS

3 TABLESPOONS CORNSTARCH

I CUP WHOLE OR 2% MILK

3 TABLESPOONS UNSALTED BUTTER

½ CUP FIRMLY PACKED DARK BROWN SUGAR

I CUP HEAVY CREAM

I TEASPOON SEA SALT, SUCH AS FLEUR DE SEL OR MALDEN SEA SALT

Savoiardi

WITH STRAWBERRIES & MASCARPONE MOUSSE

Savoiardi are the crisp Italian ladyfinger cookies used in tiramisu, but they don't have to be limited to that dessert. Garnish dishes of balsamic-marinated strawberries and light mascarpone mousse with the cookies and use them to scoop up the fruit and cream. Reach for a good-quality balsamic vinegar, not the cheap stuff from the supermarket, for the smoothest flavor. Leave the mascarpone on the counter for 10 minutes to soften up before whipping it into the cream for mousse without lumps.

1. Combine the strawberries, 2 tablespoons of the sugar, the vinegar, and pepper in a medium bowl and let stand, stirring a few times, until the sugar is dissolved, 10 to 15 minutes.

2. Combine the heavy cream and remaining 1 tablespoon sugar in a medium bowl and whip with an electric mixer on high until the cream just holds soft peaks. Add the mascarpone and continue to whip until smooth.

3. Spoon some of the strawberries into each of 4 dessert goblets. Add a dollop of mousse to each goblet. Garnish each portion with a cookie and serve immediately.

Serves 4

1 PINT FRESH STRAWBERRIES, HULLED AND THINLY SLICED

3 TABLESPOONS GRANULATED SUGAR

2 TEASPOONS BALSAMIC VINEGAR

1/2 TEASPOON FRESHLY GROUND BLACK PEPPER

1/2 CUP COLD HEAVY CREAM

1/2 CUP MASCARPONE, SOFTENED

4 SAVOIARDI COOKIES

Parfaits

You may not be able to identify the white chocolate added to this tapioca, but it gives the pudding its creamy richness. Layered with mango and topped with a few sparkling pieces of crystallized ginger, it becomes a dinner party–worthy dessert.

1. In a medium-size, heavy saucepan, whisk the tapioca, milk, eggs, sugar, and salt. Let stand until the tapioca begins to swell, about 5 minutes.

2. Bring the tapioca to a boil over medium-high heat, whisking constantly. Reduce the heat to medium low and cook, whisking constantly, until slightly thickened, about 1 minute. Remove from the heat and stir in the vanilla and chocolate until the chocolate is melted and incorporated. Set the saucepan in a bowl of ice water and stir often until cool and thick, 5 to 10 minutes.

3. Combine the mango and lime juice in a small bowl. Spoon half of the diced mango into 4 parfait glasses and top with half of the cooled tapioca. Repeat with the remaining mango and tapioca. Garnish each parfait with 2 slices of crystallized ginger and serve.

Serves 4

3 TABLESPOONS QUICK-COOKING TAPIOCA

2 CUPS WHOLE OR 2% MILK

2 LARGE EGGS, LIGHTLY BEATEN

1/4 CUP GRANULATED SUGAR

1/4 TEASPOON SALT

1 TEASPOON VANILLA EXTRACT

2 OUNCES WHITE CHOCOLATE, FINELY CHOPPED

1 MEDIUM-SIZE RIPE MANGO, PEELED AND CUT OFF THE PIT INTO 1/4-INCH DICE

1 TEASPOON FRESH LIME JUICE

8 THIN SLICES CRYSTALLIZED GINGER FOR GARNISH

Crème Fraîche Tapioca

WITH ONE-INGREDIENT RASPBERRY SAUCE

Crème fraîche gives plain tapioca a subtle tang. Serve with a minimalist's dream sauce: a bag of frozen raspberries (and nothing else!) puréed and strained.

1. In a medium-size, heavy saucepan, whisk the tapioca, milk, beaten eggs, 2 tablespoons of the honey, the sugar, and the salt. Let stand until the tapioca begins to swell, about 5 minutes.

2. Bring the tapioca to a boil over medium-high heat, whisking constantly. Reduce the heat to medium low and cook, whisking constantly, until slightly thickened, about 1 minute. Remove from the heat and stir in the vanilla. Set the saucepan in a bowl of ice water and stir often until cool and thick, about 5 minutes.

3. While the tapioca is cooling, make the raspberry sauce. Put the raspberries in a blender or food processor and process until smooth. Push the mixture through a fine mesh strainer; discard the seeds.

4. Whisk the crème fraîche into the tapioca, spoon into dessert goblets, and top with the raspberry sauce.

Serves 4

3 TABLESPOONS QUICK-COOKING TAPIOCA

2 CUPS WHOLE OR 2% MILK

2 LARGE EGGS, LIGHTLY BEATEN

¼ CUP HONEY

2 TABLESPOONS GRANULATED SUGAR

¼ TEASPOON SALT

1 TEASPOON VANILLA EXTRACT

ONE 12-OUNCE BAG FROZEN SWEETENED RASPBERRIES, THAWED

½ CUP CRÈME FRAÎCHE OR SOUR CREAM (NOT LOW- OR REDUCED-FAT)

Couscous Pudding

WITH PLUMPED BRANDIED PRUNES

*Quicker than rice pudding (you can have this on the table in 15 minutes flat)
and just as comforting, this dessert made with couscous can be varied to suit your menu.
The brandied prunes and chopped walnuts are vaguely French, but you can substitute
apricots and pistachios for a North African flavor, or cranberries and pecans
in a nod to classic American home cooking.*

1. Combine the prunes, brandy, 1 tablespoon of the sugar, and the walnuts in a small microwave-safe bowl and cover with plastic wrap. Microwave on high for 1 minute. Let stand on the counter to steep, covered, for 15 minutes.
2. Combine 1½ cups of the half-and-half, the remaining ⅓ cup sugar, and the salt in a large, heavy saucepan and bring to a boil. Stir in the couscous and cover. Take the pan off the heat and let stand for 5 minutes.
3. Meanwhile, put the egg yolks in a medium bowl. Bring the remaining 1½ cups half-and-half to a boil in a small saucepan. Whisk about ½ cup of the half-and-half into the yolks, 1 tablespoon at a time. Slowly whisk the remaining half-and-half into the egg yolks. Whisk the hot egg yolk mixture into the couscous. Turn the heat to medium high and cook, stirring constantly, until the pudding just starts to thicken, about 2 minutes.
4. Spoon the hot couscous pudding into bowls, top with the prunes, and serve.

Serves 6

1 CUP PRUNES (ABOUT 12)

¼ CUP BRANDY

⅓ CUP PLUS 1 TABLESPOON GRANULATED SUGAR

¼ CUP WALNUT PIECES, FINELY CHOPPED

3 CUPS HALF-AND-HALF

⅛ TEASPOON SALT

1 CUP COUSCOUS

2 LARGE EGG YOLKS

1 TEASPOON VANILLA EXTRACT

Bread Pudding

Baking these bread puddings in shallow crème brûlée dishes helps them to cook quickly, and they're delicious served hot from the oven. The croissants should be a day old, the better to absorb the custard mixture. If yours are fresh, tear them into pieces and dry them out in a 300-degree oven for 10 minutes before proceeding with the recipe. Croissants vary in size from bakery to bakery, so for the sake of accuracy I recommend you weigh yours to see how much you really need.

1. Preheat the oven to 350 degrees. Arrange four crème brûlée dishes or 6-ounce ramekins on a baking sheet.

2. Tear the croissants into 1-inch pieces and arrange half of the pieces in the dishes or ramekins. Sprinkle with the chocolate chips. Top with the remaining croissant pieces.

3. In a medium bowl, whisk the whole egg, egg yolk, sugar, and half-and-half and pour over the croissants. Dot each pudding with the butter. Put the baking sheet in the oven and bake the puddings until set, about 15 minutes. Serve warm or let stand for an hour and serve at room temperature.

Serves 4

4 DAY-OLD CROISSANTS (ABOUT 2 OUNCES EACH)

2/3 CUP MINI SEMISWEET CHOCOLATE CHIPS

1 LARGE EGG

1 LARGE EGG YOLK

6 TABLESPOONS GRANULATED SUGAR

2/3 CUP HALF-AND-HALF

1 TABLESPOON UNSALTED BUTTER, CUT INTO TINY PIECES

Passionfruit Fool

A classic fruit fool recipe can be made more interesting by substituting an exotic fruit like pineapple, mango, or passionfruit for strawberries or blueberries. But some of these fruits can be difficult to find at the market and difficult to prepare once you get them home. Peeling a pineapple can be downright dangerous. If you've never pitted a mango, seeded a papaya, or removed the pulp from passionfruit, you won't want to learn as you are trying to put together a 30-minute dessert. Using a frozen fruit purée (I like Goya® brand) is one way to avoid worry and hassle. Passionfruit, sweet but acidic, is my favorite, but feel free to substitute other fruit purées you think you might like, adjusting the sugar in the recipe to taste.

1. Combine the passionfruit purée and ½ cup of the sugar in a medium bowl and whisk to dissolve the sugar.
2. Combine the heavy cream and remaining ¼ cup sugar in a large bowl and whip with an electric mixer on high until the cream holds stiff peaks. Fold the passionfruit mixture into the cream. Spoon into 6 dessert goblets, garnish with the raspberries, and serve immediately. (This will keep in the refrigerator for up to 6 hours. Rewhisk briefly before serving if any liquid has separated from the fool.)

Serves 6

ONE 14-OUNCE PACKAGE UNSWEETENED PASSIONFRUIT PURÉE, THAWED

¾ CUP GRANULATED SUGAR

2 CUPS COLD HEAVY CREAM

½ CUP FRESH RASPBERRIES, PICKED OVER

QUICK TREATS WITH FROZEN FRUIT PURÉES

Once you've made a Passionfruit Fool with thawed frozen fruit purée, you may want to explore these other ways to use purées:

Agua Fresca Make great tropical drinks by pouring ½ cup of fruit purée (try pineapple, mango, or passionfruit) with 3 tablespoons light rum into a shaker filled with ice, then straining it into a chilled glass. Makes 1 drink.

Tropical Shakes Blend 1½ cups softened vanilla ice cream with 1 ½ cups fruit purée, 2 tablespoons granulated sugar, and 1 cup crushed ice until smooth. Makes 2 shakes.

Fruit Coulis Push one 14-ounce package thawed fruit purée through a fine mesh strainer into a bowl. Stir in 1 tablespoon fresh lime juice and confectioners' sugar to taste. Serve over ice cream, waffles, pound cake, or shortcakes with whipped cream.

Blackberry Fools

IN WHITE CHOCOLATE SHELLS

Take care to coat the muffin liners evenly with chocolate. If some spots are too thin,
the shells might crack and break when the liners are peeled away. If the bottoms are
too thick, they are difficult to eat neatly.

1. Line a 6-cup muffin tin with foil muffin liners. Lightly coat the inside of the liners with nonstick cooking spray.

2. Put the chocolate in a medium microwave-safe bowl and microwave on high until melted, 2 to 2½ minutes. Stir until smooth. Spoon 1 tablespoon of the melted chocolate into one of the muffin liners. Pick it up and tilt and rotate it to cover the bottom and sides with an even layer of chocolate. Place it back in the muffin tin and repeat with the remaining chocolate and cups. Place the tin in the freezer until the chocolate is set, about 10 minutes and up to 1 day.

3. Meanwhile, combine the berries and 2 tablespoons of the confectioners' sugar in a medium bowl. Stir, mashing some but not all of the berries with the back of the spoon to release some of their juices. Let stand, stirring once or twice, for 5 minutes.

4. In another medium bowl, combine the heavy cream, the remaining 1 tablespoon confectioners' sugar, and the vanilla and whip with an electric mixer on high until the cream holds soft peaks. Add the sour cream and whip on high until the mixture holds stiff peaks. Fold the berry mixture into the cream.

5. Peel the paper from the shells, spoon the mousse into the chocolate cups, and serve immediately.

Serves 6

NONSTICK COOKING SPRAY

8 OUNCES WHITE CHOCOLATE, FINELY CHOPPED

1½ CUPS FRESH BLACKBERRIES; PLUS MORE FOR GARNISH

3 tablespoons CONFECTIONERS' SUGAR; MORE TO TASTE

²⁄₃ CUP COLD HEAVY CREAM

½ TEASPOON VANILLA EXTRACT

2 TABLESPOONS SOUR CREAM (NOT LOW- OR REDUCED-FAT)

Chapter 5

Fruit
WITHOUT LABOR

For many lazy cooks, a bowl of cherries or a farmstand peach is dessert bliss. Why work when you can simply purchase some of nature's bounty and call it a day? But there's no glory in arranging a bowl of apples. People might ask you where you bought them, or whether they are Empires or Honey Crisps, but they won't be showering you with compliments for your skill and creativity. But if you take 20 minutes to stuff them with nuts and raisins, bathe them in maple syrup, pop them in the microwave, and serve them *à la mode*, then you, and not Mother Nature, will be collecting the accolades.

This chapter contains recipes for simple fruit desserts that will delight and impress. Think of fruit as a convenience product. Instead of starting from scratch, the way you must when you bake a cake, you begin with something that's already sweet and delicious, and just needs a little embellishment to take it over the top. Be sure to shop wisely and locally, if possible, for your fruit. Buy your apples in the fall from a nearby farm where they've just been picked. Seek out peaches and berries from local orchards in the summertime. Learn how to choose fruit shipped from far away. Mangos should yield slightly to the touch without being mushy; raspberries in their prime are never a dull shade of red; golden pineapples from Costa Rica are never bad. When in doubt, go with dried fruit. Dried apricots plumped and sweetened during cooking make a better dessert than rock-hard "fresh" apricots that were picked two weeks ago, well before they were ready to eat, and shipped across the country only sit in the supermarket for another week.

One of the first recipes in the chapter, sliced mango bathed in honey-sweetened coconut milk, shows that, with a minimum of handling, ripe fruit can become an extraordinary dessert. Cantaloupe drizzled with red wine syrup and sautéed peaches flambéed with a little bit of brandy prove the point twice more.

To truly transform fruit into nature's candy, just combine it with some chocolate. Everyone has had chocolate-covered strawberries, but grapes dipped in bittersweet chocolate are fun and unexpected. Or let your guests do the work, by setting out white chocolate fondue with sliced peaches or chocolate-coconut fondue with pineapple and banana.

For a more sophisticated presentation, pair fruit with cheese. Whether it's goat cheese with sautéed pears and honey, gorgonzola dolce with apricots in orange syrup, or roasted figs with fresh ricotta, the sum will be greater than the parts.

The chapter ends with several fruit gratin recipes, magical in their simplicity. To make a gratin, you arrange some fruit in a shallow baking dish, cover it with a sweetened topping, and briefly broil it to warm the fruit and caramelize the sugar. Uncooked, the fruit maintains its firmness, but the caramelized sugar lends the fruit the flavor benefits of cooking.

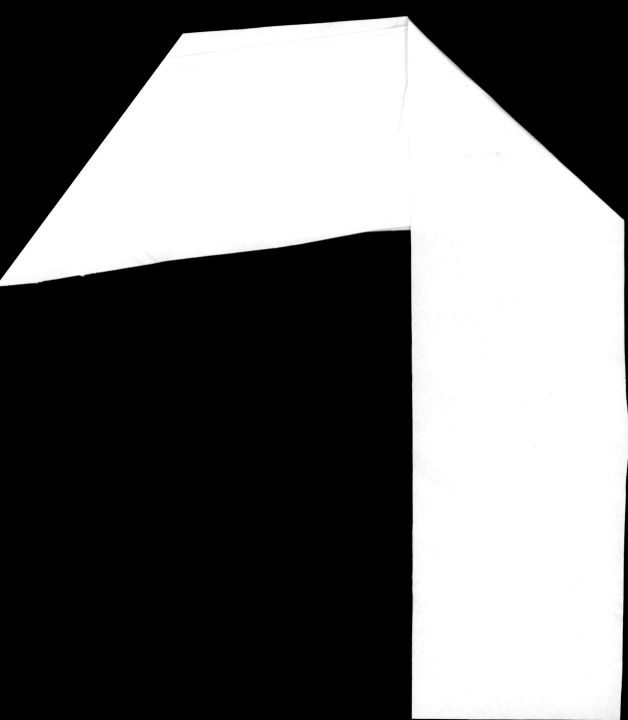

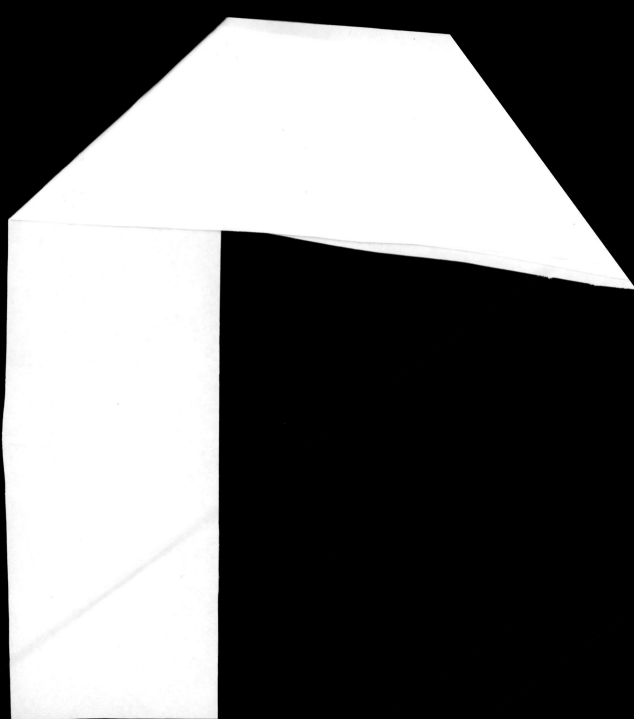

Flambéed Peaches

Here is a beautiful and easy late-summer dessert. The peaches become soft and caramelized as they cook, while the berries stay tart and firm. Flambéing is fun, but if you prefer you can skip the brandy and serve alcohol-free caramelized peaches.

1. Combine the butter and brown sugar in a large skillet and place over medium heat until the butter is melted and the sugar dissolved. Add the peaches and cook, turning often, until they've released their juices and are softened but not mushy, 4 to 5 minutes.

2. Remove the pan from the heat and sprinkle the brandy over the peaches. Tilt the pan so the liquid collects on one side. Using a long kitchen match and keeping long hair and dangling sleeves out of harm's way, ignite the brandy. Carefully return the pan to the heat and cook until the flames die down on their own, 30 seconds to 1 minute.

3. Spoon the peaches and sauce into 4 dessert dishes, then top each portion with a small scoop of ice cream and a sprinkling of berries and serve immediately.

Serves 4

3 TABLESPOONS UNSALTED BUTTER

1/2 CUP FIRMLY PACKED LIGHT BROWN SUGAR

4 RIPE BUT FIRM PEACHES, PITTED AND CUT INTO 1/2-INCH-THICK WEDGES

1/4 CUP BRANDY

1 CUP VANILLA ICE CREAM, SLIGHTLY SOFTENED

1 CUP FRESH BLUEBERRIES, PICKED OVER FOR STEMS

Mango

IN COCONUT MILK

This is such a perfect summer dessert, refreshing after some spicy barbecue. Store your mangos in the refrigerator for a few hours before you need them, if you can, to make the dessert especially cooling. You can use regular coconut milk if you like, but "lite" coconut milk is less rich and won't overwhelm the mango.

1. In a medium bowl, whisk the coconut milk, honey, and lime juice. Put the bowl in the freezer for 20 minutes to chill. (This mixture can be refrigerated for up to 1 day. Rewhisk before proceeding.)
2. Meanwhile, peel, pit, and cut the mangoes into ½-inch chunks. Divide among 6 dessert bowls. Pour some of the chilled coconut milk mixture over each portion. Garnish with mint leaves and serve.

Serves 6

ONE 13.5-OUNCE CAN UNSWEETENED "LITE" COCONUT MILK

¼ CUP HONEY

1 TABLESPOON FRESH LIME JUICE

3 RIPE MANGOS

FRESH MINT LEAVES FOR GARNISH

HOW TO PEEL AND PIT A MANGO

A mango is a mystery to anyone who has never peeled one. It conceals an irregularly shaped pit that can only be separated from the flesh with a steady hand and a sharp knife. Here are instructions for beginners:

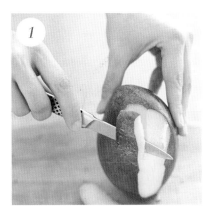

Hold the mango in one hand, resting the stem end on the cutting board. With a sharp knife in the other hand, remove strips of skin, top to bottom, working around the fruit until all the skin is removed.

Cut the flesh from the pit, again slicing from top to bottom, cutting all the way around the pit.

Then, slice into either thin strips or dice.

Cantaloupe

WITH RED WINE SYRUP

*Chilling the bowls in the freezer will make this dessert even more refreshing
as you enjoy it on a warm summer night.*

1. Put 4 dessert bowls in the freezer to chill.
2. Combine the wine and sugar in a small, heavy saucepan and bring to a boil. Cook at a lively simmer until the wine is reduced to about ¼ cup, about 10 minutes. Set the saucepan in a bowl of ice water to cool, about 15 minutes.
3. While the syrup is cooling, cut the cantaloupes in half and remove the seeds. Use a melon baller to scoop the melon flesh from the rind.
4. When you're ready to serve, divide the melon balls among the 4 chilled dessert bowls. Drizzle the cooled syrup over the melon, garnish with a basil leaf, and serve immediately.

Serves 4

1 **CUP** DRY RED WINE

2 **TABLESPOONS** GRANULATED SUGAR

2 RIPE CANTALOUPES

4 LARGE FRESH BASIL LEAVES

Caramel Baked Apples

*Making these apples in the microwave cuts the baking time dramatically.
You can vary the filling by using different types of nuts or by substituting raisins
for a portion of the nuts. The juices thicken into a delicious sauce and can be spooned
over the ice cream and apples before serving.*

1. Use a vegetable peeler to remove top third of each apple skin. Use a sharp paring knife to remove the core of each apple, leaving the bottom end intact. Scrape away any remaining bits of core and seeds with a spoon.

2. Combine the walnuts, brown sugar, and butter in a small bowl and mash with a fork until the mixture comes together in coarse crumbs. Tightly pack the apples with the mixture.

3. Arrange the apples in a microwave-safe baking dish so they're not touching one another. Drape with plastic wrap and microwave until they're soft when pierced with a skewer, 5 to 7 minutes, depending on the power and size of your microwave. Carefully remove the plastic (there will be steam, which can scald you) and let cool for 10 minutes.

4. Place each apple in a dessert bowl along with a scoop of ice cream. Drizzle the juices from the baking dish over the apples and ice cream, if desired. Serve immediately.

Serves 4

4 GRANNY SMITH APPLES

1/2 CUP CHOPPED WALNUTS

1/4 CUP FIRMLY PACKED LIGHT BROWN SUGAR

1 TABLESPOON UNSALTED BUTTER, CUT INTO BITS

1 PINT VANILLA ICE CREAM, SLIGHTLY SOFTENED

Roasted Figs

& RICOTTA CHEESE

*Fresh figs make only brief appearances at the market, so when I see them
I snap them up to make this lovely summer dessert.*

1. Preheat the oven to 400 degrees.
2. Slice the figs in half lengthwise from end to end. Place them cut side up in a shallow baking dish. Sprinkle each half with ½ teaspoon of the brown sugar. Bake until softened and caramelized, 5 to 7 minutes. Remove from the oven and let cool for 5 minutes.
3. Divide the ricotta among 4 dessert bowls. Top each portion with 3 fig halves and serve immediately.

Serves 4

12 RIPE, FRESH FIGS, WIPED CLEAN

¼ CUP FIRMLY PACKED LIGHT BROWN SUGAR

2 CUPS WHOLE-MILK RICOTTA CHEESE

Chocolate-Covered Grapes

*If you adore chocolate-covered strawberries, you will love these grapes. They're especially
pretty when served in small clusters. Your grapes should be completely dry and well chilled
when you dip them in the chocolate, to ensure a nice chocolate finish.*

1. Line a large baking sheet with parchment or waxed paper. Use
   a scissor to snip the grapes into small bunches. Put them in the
   freezer while the chocolate melts.
2. In a medium saucepan, bring 2 inches of water to a bare simmer.
   Put the chocolate in a stainless-steel bowl big enough to rest
   on top of the saucepan and set it over the pan, making sure it
   doesn't touch the water. Heat, whisking occasionally, until most
   of the chocolate is melted. Remove from the heat and whisk
   until smooth.
3. Hold a bunch of grapes by the stem over the bowl of chocolate.
   Use a spoon to spoon chocolate over the grapes to coat them
   completely, letting the excess drip back into the bowl. Place on
   the prepared baking sheet and repeat with the remaining grapes.
   Freeze for 10 minutes and serve, or refrigerate for up to 1 day
   before serving.

Serves 4

1 POUND SEEDLESS GRAPES

1/2 POUND BEST-QUALITY
BITTERSWEET, MILK, OR WHITE
CHOCOLATE, COARSELY CHOPPED

Tropical Fruit

WITH CHOCOLATE-COCONUT FONDUE

Here is an especially easy and flavorful variation on chocolate fondue.
Any extra sauce can be refrigerated and rewarmed before being spooned over ice cream.

1. Combine the cream of coconut and cocoa in a small, heavy saucepan. Set over low heat and whisk until the mixture is warmed through and smooth.

2. Transfer the mixture to a fondue pot or a warmed heatproof bowl, stir in the extracts and salt, and serve with the mango, bananas, and pineapple for dipping.

Serves 6

ONE 15-OUNCE CAN CREAM OF COCONUT, SUCH AS COCO LOPEZ

6 TABLESPOONS UNSWEETENED COCOA POWER

1/2 TEASPOON VANILLA EXTRACT

1/2 TEASPOON COCONUT EXTRACT

1/8 TEASPOON SALT

1 RIPE MANGO, PEELED, PITTED, AND CUT INTO 1-INCH CHUNKS

2 RIPE BANANAS, PEELED AND CUT INTO 1-INCH-THICK SLICES

3 CUPS 1-INCH CHUNKS FRESH PINEAPPLE

Peaches

WITH WHITE CHOCOLATE FONDUE

White chocolate is a good match with summery peaches. For a nonalcoholic version, substitute ½ teaspoon vanilla extract for the brandy. Don't worry if you don't have a fondue pot. Warm a heatproof bowl in a 180-degree oven for 10 minutes and transfer the fondue to the bowl. The chocolate will stay warm for about 20 minutes this way.

1. Combine the chocolate and heavy cream in a small, heavy saucepan. Set over low heat and whisk until the chocolate is melted and the mixture is smooth.
2. Transfer the melted chocolate to a fondue pot or a warmed heatproof bowl, using a rubber spatula to get it all out, stir in the brandy, and serve with the peaches for dipping.

Serves 6

12 OUNCES WHITE CHOCOLATE, COARSELY CHOPPED

3/4 CUP HEAVY CREAM

1 TABLESPOON BRANDY

6 FIRM BUT RIPE PEACHES, PITTED AND CUT INTO 8 WEDGES EACH

Apricots in Orange Syrup

WITH GORGONZOLA DOLCE

Gorgonzola dolce is a mild and creamy Italian blue cheese, with just enough bite to offset the sweetness of apricots in Grand Marnier® syrup. It's a wonderful pairing and proves how sophisticated and beautiful a very simple dessert can be.

1. Combine the apricots, Grand Marnier, and brown sugar in a small, heavy saucepan and bring to a simmer over medium heat. Cook, stirring a few times, until the sugar has dissolved and the liquid is syrupy, 3 to 5 minutes. Transfer to a bowl and let cool to warm room temperature.

2. Put a piece of gorgonzola on each of 4 dessert plates. Spoon some apricots and syrup alongside the cheese and serve immediately.

Serves 4

6 OUNCES (⅔ CUP) DRIED APRICOTS, COARSELY CHOPPED

½ CUP GRAND MARNIER OR OTHER ORANGE LIQUEUR

¼ CUP FIRMLY PACKED LIGHT BROWN SUGAR

6 OUNCES GORGONZOLA DOLCE

Brandied Prunes

WITH MASCARPONE

*When prunes are cooked in brandy, they become deliciously plump and juicy,
absorbing the flavors of both the brandy and lemon zest. Sitting on a pillow
of creamy, mellow mascarpone, they're irresistible.*

1. Combine the brandy, prunes, brown sugar, and lemon zest in a medium-size, heavy saucepan and bring to a simmer over medium heat. Cook until the liquid is thickened, 7 to 10 minutes. Discard the lemon zest, then transfer the mixture to a bowl and let cool for 15 minutes.

2. Place a scoop (of about 6 tablespoons each) of mascarpone in each of 4 dessert goblets. Spoon the prunes and juices over the mascarpone. Serve immediately.

Serves 4

I CUP BRANDY

I2 PITTED PRUNES

¼ CUP FIRMLY PACKED LIGHT BROWN SUGAR

ZEST FROM I LEMON, REMOVED IN A WIDE STRIP WITH A VEGETABLE PEELER

I½ CUPS MASCARPONE

Pears

*Here's another favorite fruit and cheese pairing, very light yet somehow
still indulgent, and perfect after a hearty winter meal.*

1. Put the walnuts in a small, dry skillet over medium heat and toast
   them, shaking the pan, until fragrant, 1 to 2 minutes. Transfer to a
   small bowl and stir in the honey and pepper.
2. Peel, core, and thinly slice the pears. Fan the pear slices on
   4 dessert plates. Set a piece of goat cheese alongside the pear.
   Spoon the walnut-and-honey mixture over the pears and cheese.
   Serve immediately.

Serves 4

⅓ CUP WALNUT PIECES, COARSELY
CHOPPED

½ CUP HONEY

½ TEASPOON FRESHLY GROUND
BLACK PEPPER

2 RIPE PEARS

4 OUNCES FRESH GOAT CHEESE

Strawberry Meringue Gratin

This gratin is like a meringue pie, but without the bother of a crust. To make this charming dessert, just whip egg whites and sugar, smooth over a baking dish full of strawberries, and bake until the topping is golden—about 10 minutes.

1. Preheat the oven to 375 degrees.
2. Arrange the strawberries in an even layer in a shallow 8-inch-square baking dish.
3. Combine the brown sugar and granulated sugar in a food processor and process until the sugars are finely ground.
4. Put the egg whites in a medium bowl and whip with an electric mixer on high until foamy. With the mixer running, add the ground sugar in a slow, steady stream and continue to whip until the egg whites just hold stiff peaks. Spread the meringue over the berries with a rubber spatula.
5. Put the gratin in the oven and bake until the meringue is golden brown, 10 to 12 minutes. Serve immediately.

Serves 6

1 PINT FRESH STRAWBERRIES, HULLED AND THINLY SLICED

3 TABLESPOONS FIRMLY PACKED LIGHT BROWN SUGAR

3 TABLESPOONS GRANULATED SUGAR

2 LARGE EGG WHITES

Plum & Greek Yogurt Gratins

I love creamy, thick Greek-style yogurt, which is tangy like sour cream. Mixed with honey, it makes a rich blanket for ripe sliced plums. Panko breadcrumbs, airy and light, give the gratins a nice crunch but don't weigh them down.

1. Position an oven rack as close to the heating element as possible and preheat the broiler.
2. Whisk the yogurt and honey in a small bowl. Stir the panko and brown sugar in another small bowl.
3. Divide the plums among 4 mini gratin dishes. Spoon the yogurt mixture over the plums. Set the dishes on a baking sheet and broil until the yogurt is bubbling, 1 to 2 minutes.
4. Sprinkle the panko mixture over the gratins and return to the broiler. Broil until the crumbs are browned and the brown sugar is caramelized, 2 to 3 minutes. Serve immediately.

Serves 4

1 CUP FULL-FAT PLAIN YOGURT, PREFERABLY GREEK-STYLE

¼ CUP HONEY

½ CUP JAPANESE-STYLE PANKO BREADCRUMBS

2 TABLESPOONS FIRMLY PACKED LIGHT BROWN SUGAR

8 RIPE PLUMS (ABOUT 1½ POUNDS), PITTED AND CUT INTO 6 SLICES EACH

Pineapple-Coconut Gratin

*Fresh pineapple is now available pre-peeled and pre-sliced at the supermarket,
great for quick desserts like this tropical gratin. Let it come to room temperature
before you assemble the dessert, so it warms up sufficiently under the broiler,
and serve it immediately. The warm juices from the bottom of the dish
make a delicious sauce for the ice cream.*

1. Position an oven rack as close to the heating element as possible and preheat the broiler. Brush a 9-inch glass pie plate with some of the melted butter.

2. Arrange the pineapple slices over the bottom of the pie plate. Drizzle with the remaining melted butter and sprinkle with the lime juice. Sprinkle the brown sugar over the slices. Broil until the brown sugar is bubbling, 2 to 2 ½ minutes. Sprinkle the coconut over the top, return to the broiler, and broil until golden, 15 to 30 seconds. Watch carefully because the coconut will burn quickly after it browns.

3. Put 2 pineapple slices in each of 4 dessert bowls, top with 2 small scoops of ice cream and some of the juices from the pie plate, and serve immediately.

Serves 4

2 TABLESPOONS UNSALTED BUTTER, MELTED

1 PRE-PEELED AND SLICED FRESH PINEAPPLE (ABOUT NINE ½-INCH-THICK SLICES)

2 TEASPOONS FRESH LIME JUICE

¼ CUP FIRMLY PACKED LIGHT BROWN SUGAR

¼ CUP SWEETENED FLAKED COCONUT

1 PINT VANILLA ICE CREAM, SLIGHTLY SOFTENED

Chapter 6

Ice Cream

IN AN INSTANT

With all of the super-premium ice creams now available in every supermarket and convenience store in the country, it's tempting to just scoop some Häagen Dazs® or Ciao Bella® into a bowl and call it a day. But all of those pints of Ben & Jerry's® stacked in the freezer case can be building blocks for some fun and impressive desserts. If you spend just a few minutes of extra time to produce the treats in this chapter—ice cream sandwiches, parfaits, sundaes, sodas—you'll be rewarded for your "work" with smiles all around.

Pick up some coffee ice cream, then stroll down the cookie aisle for some chocolate wafer cookies, and grab a couple of milk chocolate and toffee candy bars at the checkout counter. Congratulations, you've done most of the work required to make Mini Coffee-Toffee Ice Cream Sandwiches.

Want to riff on the classic ice cream-and-waffle cone combination? Construct a parfait with Belgian butter waffle cookies and ice cream, topped off with strawberries and whipped cream.

Or get saucy. Sprinkle vanilla ice cream with Raisinets® and pour on a rich, warm sauce made with heavy cream, chocolate, and peanut butter. Top a tropical banana split with caramel-mango sauce made by cooking frozen mango purée with dark brown sugar.

Sundaes too decadent? Go for a fresh fruit and ice cream combination. Kumquat compote is delicious over chocolate ice cream, as are chunks of seedless watermelon.

And if you're really lazy, you can always drink your dessert through a straw. Try Blackbottom Grasshopper Milkshakes, made with chocolate and mint chocolate chip ice cream. And remember that ice cream drinks aren't just for kids. Serve the Tequila & Orange Ice Cream Sodas to the grown-ups.

Ice cream isn't just a weeknight fallback or casual entertaining staple. For the most festive and celebratory occasions, Raspberry & Champagne Ice Cream Floats will hit the spot with a lot of bubbles but no fuss at all.

Ice Cream Sandwiches

Nabisco Famous Chocolate Wafers make wonderful mini ice cream sandwiches, perfect for pulling out of the freezer after a summer barbecue. Let your ice cream soften for a few minutes on the counter before using it, but don't let it get too soft (the microwave works well if your ice cream is rock hard; start by microwaving on high for 10 seconds, then test by inserting a knife into the center of the container). And work quickly, placing each sandwich in the freezer as soon as you've put it together.

1. Put the candy bits in a shallow bowl.
2. Use a ¼-cup ice cream scoop or dry measure to measure out ¼ cup of ice cream and sandwich it between two of the wafer cookies, gently pressing them together so the ice cream comes to the edges of the cookies.
3. Roll the edges of the sandwich in the candy bits to coat the exposed ice cream. Put the sandwich on a baking sheet in the freezer. Repeat with the remaining cookies, ice cream, and candy until you have 8 sandwiches.
4. Cover the baking sheet with plastic wrap and return it to the freezer until ready to serve, at least 15 minutes and up to 3 days.

Makes 8

TWO 1.4-OUNCE MILK CHOCOLATE AND TOFFEE BARS SUCH AS SKOR®, FINELY CHOPPED

1 PINT COFFEE ICE CREAM, SLIGHTLY SOFTENED

16 NABISCO FAMOUS CHOCOLATE WAFERS

IMPROVISING
ICE CREAM SANDWICHES

Using the same proportion of ice cream and candy or nut coating to cookies as in the recipes in this chapter, you can come up with your own ice cream sandwich combinations. Here are some more ideas to get you started:

* Mint chocolate chip ice cream, chopped Andes® Mint candies, and chocolate wafer cookies

* Peanut butter cup ice cream, chopped Butterfingers® candy bars, and chocolate wafer cookies

* Rum raisin ice cream, chopped walnuts, and butter waffle cookies

* Mango sorbet, toasted flaked coconut, and gingersnaps

* Peach ice cream, sliced almonds, and gingersnaps spread with a little bit of peach preserves

CHOCOLATE-CHERRY

Butter Waffle Sandwiches

I've been using Belgian butter waffle cookies to garnish bowls of ice cream for years, but just realized that they're a natural for ice cream sandwiches. Their pure vanilla flavor is wonderful with cherry vanilla ice cream. To garnish, I chop chocolate-covered dried cherries to coat the ice cream edges.

1. Put the chopped cherries in a shallow bowl.
2. Use a ¼-cup ice cream scoop or dry measure to measure out ¼ cup of ice cream and sandwich it between two of the waffle cookies, gently pressing them together so the ice cream comes to the edges of the cookies.
3. Roll the edges of the sandwich in the cherries to coat the exposed ice cream. Put the sandwich on a baking sheet in the freezer. Repeat with the remaining cookies, ice cream, and cherries until you have 4 sandwiches.
4. Cover the baking sheet with plastic wrap and return it to the freezer until ready to serve, at least 15 minutes and up to 3 days.

Makes 4

½ CUP CHOCOLATE-COVERED DRIED CHERRIES, CHOPPED

1 PINT CHERRY VANILLA ICE CREAM, SLIGHTLY SOFTENED

8 BELGIAN BUTTER WAFFLE COOKIES, SUCH AS JULES DESTROOPER

Ice Cream Sandwiches

I've seen recipes similar to this one using homemade cookies and ice cream,
and I think this shortcut version is just as good. Use sturdier gingersnaps here—
thin cookies will break into pieces.

1. Put the chopped pistachios in a shallow bowl.
2. Put the ice cream in a large bowl, sprinkle with the lemon zest and cranberries, and use the back of a large spoon to mash it all together. Place in the freezer for 10 minutes to firm up.
3. Use ¼-cup ice cream scoop or dry measure to measure out ¼ cup of ice cream and sandwich it between two of the gingersnaps, gently pressing them together so the ice cream comes to the edges of the cookies.
4. Roll the edges of the sandwich in the pistachios to coat the exposed ice cream. Put the sandwich on a baking sheet in the freezer. Repeat with the remaining cookies, ice cream, and nuts until you have 8 sandwiches.
5. Cover the baking sheet with plastic wrap and return to the freezer until ready to serve, at least 15 minutes and up to 3 days.

Makes 8

½ CUP SHELLED UNSALTED PISTACHIOS, FINELY CHOPPED

1 PINT VANILLA ICE CREAM, SLIGHTLY SOFTENED

2 TEASPOONS FINELY GRATED LEMON ZEST

⅓ CUP DRIED CRANBERRIES, CHOPPED

16 GINGERSNAP COOKIES

Ice Cream Sundae Cones

Ice cream cones dipped in chocolate, rolled in sprinkles, and topped with a maraschino cherry are a fun substitute for sundaes in dishes. Mix and match your ice cream flavors and dark, milk, and white chocolate coatings as you like. Chopped nuts may be substituted for the sprinkles.

1. Carefully fill each cone with about 1 tablespoon ice cream, then top it with a ¼-cup scoop of ice cream. Press down gently on the ice cream with the back of the scoop to make sure that the ice cream is secure in the cone. Place each filled cone upright in a small juice glass, put the juice glasses on a baking sheet, and set in the freezer until the ice cream is firm, at least 15 minutes and up to 3 hours.

2. Meanwhile, fill a medium saucepan with 2 inches of water and bring to a bare simmer. Combine the chocolate and oil in a stainless-steel bowl big enough to rest on top of the saucepan. Set the bowl over the simmering water, making sure that the bottom of the bowl doesn't touch the water. Heat, whisking occasionally, until the chocolate is completely melted. Remove from the heat and set aside to cool until just lukewarm.

3. Put the sprinkles in a small bowl. Remove one of the cones from the freezer and, working over the bowl of chocolate, spoon chocolate over the ice cream, coating it completely and letting any excess drip back into the bowl. Hold the cone over the bowl of sprinkles and lightly spoon the sprinkles over the cone. Dip the bottom of one cherry in the chocolate and press it into the top of the cone. Stand the cone back in the juice glass and return it to the freezer. Repeat with the remaining cones, chocolate, sprinkles, and cherries. Freeze until the chocolate is firm, at least 5 minutes and up to 6 hours.

Makes 8

8 SUGAR CONES

1 PINT PLUS ½ CUP ICE CREAM OF YOUR CHOICE, SLIGHTLY SOFTENED

12 OUNCES SEMISWEET CHOCOLATE, FINELY CHOPPED

2½ TABLESPOONS VEGETABLE OIL

¼ CUP MULTICOLORED SPRINKLES

8 MARASCHINO CHERRIES WITH STEMS

Raisinet Ice Cream Parfaits

WITH CHOCOLATE-PEANUT BUTTER SAUCE

Chocolate–peanut butter sauce is simple to make and a fun variation on hot fudge. Use it in this simple parfait of ice cream layered with chopped Raisinets candies when you want an ice cream dessert with classic flavors but an unexpected presentation.

1. Combine 1 cup of the heavy cream, the chocolate, and peanut butter in a medium-size, heavy saucepan, set over medium heat, and whisk until the chocolate is melted and the mixture is smooth. Set aside to cool slightly.

2. Combine the remaining ½ cup cream and the confectioners' sugar in a medium bowl and whip with an electric mixer on high until the cream just holds stiff peaks.

3. Put 2 small scoops of ice cream (about 2 tablespoons each) in each of 4 parfait glasses and sprinkle with about 1 tablespoon of the chocolate-covered raisins. Repeat with 2 more scoops and more raisins. Top each sundae with the warm chocolate–peanut butter sauce, then the whipped cream. Sprinkle a couple of chocolate-covered raisins on top and serve immediately.

Serves 4

1½ CUPS HEAVY CREAM

5 OUNCES MILK CHOCOLATE, FINELY CHOPPED

3 TABLESPOONS SMOOTH PEANUT BUTTER

1 TABLESPOON CONFECTIONERS' SUGAR

1 PINT VANILLA ICE CREAM, SLIGHTLY SOFTENED

ONE 3.5-OUNCE BOX (ABOUT ½ CUP) Raisinet CHOCOLATE-COVERED RAISINS, COARSELY CHOPPED

Ice Cream Parfaits

*Think of this as a neater and more dignified way of eating an ice cream cone: Break up
butter waffle cookies, layer them with ice cream, and eat the whole thing with a spoon.
Another advantage to this presentation—you can add Grand Marnier and whipped
cream, neither of which can be used to top an ice cream cone!*

1. Combine the strawberries, 1 tablespoon of the sugar, and the Grand Marnier in a small bowl and let stand, stirring occasionally, until the sugar is dissolved, about 5 minutes.

2. Put a small scoop of ice cream (about 2 tablespoons) in each of 4 parfait glasses, sprinkle with the cookie pieces, and top with the strawberries and liqueur. Place in the freezer while you whip the cream.

3. In a medium bowl, whip the heavy cream and the remaining 1 tablespoon sugar with an electric beater on high until the cream holds stiff peaks. Remove the parfaits from the freezer and top with the whipped cream. Serve immediately.

Serves 4

1 CUP FRESH STRAWBERRIES, HULLED AND CHOPPED

2 TABLESPOONS GRANULATED SUGAR

1/4 CUP GRAND MARNIER OR OTHER ORANGE LIQUEUR

4 BUTTER WAFFLE COOKIES, SUCH AS JULES DESTROOPER, BROKEN INTO PIECES

1 PINT STRAWBERRY ICE CREAM, SLIGHTLY SOFTENED

1/2 CUP COLD HEAVY CREAM

Peaches & Ice Cream

WITH MAPLE-WALNUT SAUCE

*I ordered my fair share of ice cream sundaes at the local ice cream parlor as a kid,
and while I'd periodically change ice cream flavors from coffee to mint chocolate chip
or substitute marshmallow sauce for whipped cream, I'd always asked for "wet" walnuts.
Here's a recent favorite sundae combination—peaches and cream—with maple-flavored
wet nuts included in the mix.*

1. Preheat the oven to 350 degrees. Spread the nuts on a baking sheet and toast until fragrant, 5 to 7 minutes.

2. Combine the maple syrup, brown sugar, and ½ cup of the heavy cream in a medium-size, heavy saucepan and bring to a boil over medium heat, stirring to dissolve the sugar. Boil for 1 minute. Remove from the heat and stir in the vanilla and toasted walnuts. Set aside to cool slightly.

3. In a medium bowl, whip the remaining ½ cup cream and the confectioners' sugar with an electric mixer on high until the cream just hold stiff peaks.

4. Divide the ice cream among 4 dessert bowls. Arrange the peaches on top. Drizzle with the warm walnut sauce, top with the whipped cream, and serve immediately.

Serves 4

I CUP WALNUT PIECES

¼ CUP PURE MAPLE SYRUP

¼ CUP FIRMLY PACKED LIGHT BROWN SUGAR

I CUP HEAVY CREAM

½ TEASPOON VANILLA EXTRACT

I TABLESPOON CONFECTIONERS' SUGAR

I PINT VANILLA ICE CREAM, SLIGHTLY SOFTENED

2 MEDIUM-SIZE, RIPE PEACHES, PITTED AND CUT INTO ½-INCH-THICK WEDGES

Sundaes

*Watermelon, bittersweet chocolate, and anisette combine in an intriguing way in this
simple but sophisticated parfait dessert. The ice cream adds luxurious creaminess,
completing the combination.*

1. Divide the watermelon among 4 dessert goblets. Drizzle 1 table-spoon of the anisette over each portion, then sprinkle with some of the chocolate. Top with a ¼-cup scoop of ice cream and sprinkle over the remaining chocolate. Serve immediately.

Makes 4

ONE 4-POUND PIECE SEEDLESS WATERMELON, RIND REMOVED, FLESH CUT INTO 1-INCH CHUNKS

¼ CUP ANISETTE OR OTHER ANISE LIQUEUR

2 OUNCES BITTERSWEET CHOCOLATE, SHAVED (YOU CAN DO THIS WITH A VEGETABLE PEELER)

1 CUP VANILLA ICE CREAM, SLIGHTLY SOFTENED

Banana Splits

WITH MANGO-CARAMEL SAUCE

An unusual and delicious dessert sauce, made by cooking mango purée with dark brown sugar, tops these tropical-themed banana splits. Keep any extra mango-caramel sauce in the refrigerator in an airtight container for up to 1 week and rewarm it in the microwave.

1. Put the coconut in a small, dry skillet and toast over medium heat, shaking often, until golden, 2 to 3 minutes. Transfer to a bowl to cool.

2. Combine the brown sugar and mango purée in a medium-size, heavy saucepan and bring to a boil over medium heat. Boil until thickened and reduced to 1¼ cups, 10 to 12 minutes. Stir in the butter and rum and transfer to a heatproof glass measuring cup to cool for 15 minutes.

3. In a medium bowl, whip the heavy cream and sugar with an electric mixer on high until the cream just holds stiff peaks.

4. Peel, then split the bananas in half lengthwise and arrange in 4 banana split dishes. Top each portion with 3 small scoops of ice cream, spoon over the warm mango sauce, top with the whipped cream, and garnish with the coconut and the star fruit slices. Serve immediately.

Makes 4

½ CUP SWEETENED FLAKED COCONUT

½ CUP FIRMLY PACKED DARK BROWN SUGAR

ONE 14-OUNCE PACKAGE FROZEN MANGO PURÉE, THAWED

2 TABLESPOONS UNSALTED BUTTER

2 TABLESPOONS DARK RUM

¾ CUP HEAVY CREAM

3 TABLESPOONS GRANULATED SUGAR

4 SMALL, RIPE BANANAS

1 PINT VANILLA ICE CREAM, SLIGHTLY SOFTENED

2 STAR FRUITS, CUT INTO ¼-INCH-THICK SLICES

Grasshopper Milkshakes

Here I make two separate milkshake mixtures and layer them in one glass. Serve them right after you pour them if you want your guests to appreciate the visual effect, since the green and brown parts will start to blend together in a minute or two!

1. Put ½ cup of the milk, the mint chocolate chip ice cream, and crème de menthe in a blender and blend until just smooth. Pour into a measuring cup.

2. Rinse out the blender and put the remaining ½ cup milk, the chocolate ice cream, and chocolate syrup in the blender and blend until just smooth. Pour the chocolate milkshake mixture into four 8-ounce glasses and top with the mint milkshake mixture. Garnish with mint leaves and serve immediately.

Makes 4

1 CUP MILK

1 PINT MINT CHOCOLATE CHIP ICE CREAM, SLIGHTLY SOFTENED

¼ CUP CRÈME DE MENTHE LIQUEUR

1 PINT CHOCOLATE ICE CREAM, SLIGHTLY SOFTENED

¼ CUP CHOCOLATE SYRUP

FRESH MINT LEAVES FOR GARNISH

Buttermilk Shakes

*These sweet and tart shakes are very pretty, served in juice glasses and garnished with
a small scoop of ice cream or a peach slice if you like.*

1. Combine the peaches, sugar, and schnapps in a blender and purée until smooth. Add the ice cream and buttermilk. Blend until just smooth.
2. Pour the milkshake into two 8-ounce glasses. Garnish each glass with a small scoop of ice cream. Serve immediately.

Makes 2

3 MEDIUM-SIZE RIPE PEACHES, PEELED, PITTED, AND CUT INTO 1-INCH CHUNKS

2 TABLESPOONS GRANULATED SUGAR, OR MORE TO TASTE

2 TABLESPOONS PEACH SCHNAPPS

1/2 CUP BUTTERMILK

1 PINT VANILLA ICE CREAM; PLUS MORE FOR GARNISH, SLIGHTLY SOFTENED

Mocha Kahlúa® Ice Cream Sodas

Bubbly and refreshing, ice cream sodas are lighter on the palate than milkshakes.

1. Pour 2 tablespoons of the chocolate syrup and 2 tablespoons of the club soda into each of 4 tall glasses. Stir to combine. Drop a ½-cup scoop of ice cream into each glass. Drizzle 2 tablespoons of the espresso and 2 tablespoons of the Kahlúa over each portion. Fill the remainder of each glass with club soda. Serve immediately with a straw and a long-handled spoon.

Makes 4

½ CUP CHOCOLATE SYRUP

I QUART CLUB SODA

I PINT COFFEE ICE CREAM, SLIGHTLY SOFTENED

½ CUP BREWED ESPRESSO, CHILLED

½ CUP KAHLÚA OR OTHER COFFEE LIQUEUR

Tequila-Orange Ice Cream Sodas

I use Boylan's® brand soda to make this creamsicle-inspired drink for grown-ups.

1. Put a ½-cup scoop of ice cream in each of 4 tall glasses. Drizzle 1 tablespoon of the tequila and 1 tablespoon of the Grand Marnier over each portion. Fill the remainder of each glass with orange soda. Serve immediately with a straw and a long-handled spoon.

Makes 4

I PINT VANILLA ICE CREAM, SLIGHTLY SOFTENED

¼ CUP TEQUILA

¼ CUP GRAND MARNIER OR OTHER ORANGE LIQUEUR

TWO 12-OUNCE BOTTLES CHILLED ORANGE SODA

SPIKED ICE CREAM SODAS

*Here are some more fun ways
to make grown-up ice cream sodas:*

Gin Lemonade Ice Cream Sodas Dissolve ¼ cup superfine sugar in ¼ cup fresh lemon juice. Stir in ½ cup gin. Portion into 4 tall glasses. Add ½ cup vanilla ice cream to each glass and top off each one with 1 cup club soda.

White Russian Ice Cream Sodas Put ½ cup vanilla ice cream in each of 4 tall glasses. Drizzle 2 tablespoons Kahlúa and 2 tablespoons vodka over each one. Top off each with 1 cup club soda.

Shirley Temple Ice Cream Sodas Put ½ cup cherry vanilla ice cream in each of 4 tall glasses. Drizzle 2 tablespoons kirsch over each one and top off each with 1 cup ginger ale. Garnish each with a maraschino cherry.

After Dinner Coffee Ice Cream Sodas Put ½ cup coffee ice cream in each of 4 tall glasses. Drizzle 2 tablespoons Sambuca over each one. Top off with 1 cup club soda.

Ice Cream Floats

*Here is my most elegant take on the ice cream soda, a scoop of vanilla ice cream
and a handful of raspberries floating in a glass of champagne.*

1. Put 2 tablespoons of the raspberries in the bottom of each of 4 tall glasses. Top with a ¼-cup scoop of ice cream. Drizzle 1 tablespoon framboise into each glass, then top with another 2 tablespoons of raspberries and another ¼-cup scoop of ice cream. Pour ½ cup of champagne into each glass. Serve immediately with a straw and a long-handled spoon

Makes 4

1 CUP FRESH RASPBERRIES, PICKED OVER

1 PINT VANILLA ICE CREAM, SLIGHTLY SOFTENED

¼ CUP FRAMBOISE OR OTHER RASPBERRY EAU DE VIE

2 CUPS CHILLED DRY CHAMPAGNE OR SPARKLING WINE

Chapter 7

Fleet SWEETS

Making candies and confections at home doesn't have to be an intimidating process requiring a chemistry degree or involving thermometers and marble slabs. Exclude the scary-difficult stuff—taffy, ribbon candy, old-fashioned fudge—and there are still a lot of sweets you can make in a flash and without fuss.

The recipes in this chapter come together quickly and without special equipment. Chocolate bark, truffles, nougat, nut brittle, and caramel popcorn are all doable in 30 minutes if you know a few tricks.

Often with these easy candies, the toughest thing is to get your sweets to cool down quickly enough to eat it in 30 minutes. To solidify Milk Chocolate, Peanut & Raisin Bark, you can freeze the pan before pouring the melted chocolate into it. It will begin to set up on contact with the cold metal. Likewise, freezing the coconut centers of Almond Joy® Bonbons before coating them with chocolate will make the chocolate set up instantly. Ganache usually needs an hour or two in the refrigerator to harden before it can be rolled into balls to make truffles. But if you make just a small amount and then let it stand in an ice bath, you can get going on the rolling in a matter of minutes.

Candy made with cooked sugar (or honey, or maple syrup) gets very, very hot, but also cools down much more quickly than chocolate candy. It's not necessary to take the temperature of your sugar, but do watch it carefully and follow the recipe closely to avoid burning it in the pan while cooking it for the recommended amount of time.

Once it's done, be sure to reased utensils and pour it onto a parchment-lined baking sheet or greas to avoid a sticky mess. I am embarrassed to say I wasted 40 minutes trying away the foil from my first batch of Greek Honey & Sesame Seed Cand one I made before I realized how essential it was to spray the foil with nostick cooking spray before doing anything else!

As with every other category of quick desserts, quick candy doesn't have to be boring. Interesting ingredients and surprising flavor combinations can elevate even the simplest recipes. White chocolate ganache is infused with green tea to produce a lovely and aromatic truffle. A few fennel seeds hidden inside a chocolate-dipped dried fig punch up the flavor of the bonbon. Kraft® caramels are not just coated with chocolate, but sprinkled with chopped smokehouse almonds, for a smoky and salty contrast.

Almond Joy Bonbons

*This connoisseur's version of a favorite candy bar is m̲ ̲ ̲th
unsweetened coconut and best-quality bittersweet ch̲ ̲ ̲ ̲.*

1. Line a baking sheet with parchment or waxed paper.
2. Combine the coconut, condensed milk, vanilla, and salt in a medium bowl. Roll tablespoonfuls of the mixture between your palms and set them on the prepared baking sheet. Put the sheet in the freezer for 5 minutes.
3. Put the chocolate in a small microwave-safe bowl and microwave on high until melted, 30 seconds to 1 minute, depending on the power and size of your microwave. Whisk until smooth.
4. Place a coconut ball on a fork and lower it into the bowl of chocolate. Turn the fork until the ball completely covered with chocolate, then lift from the bowl, letting the excess drip back into the bowl. Set the ball back on the parchment and press an almond into the top of the candy. Repeat with the remaining coconut balls.
5. Put the baking sheet back in the freezer until the chocolate is firm, about 5 minutes. The bonbons will keep in the refrigerator in an airtight container for up to 1 week.

Makes 12

1 1/2 **CUPS** UNSWEETENED FLAKED COCONUT

1/3 **CUP** SWEETENED CONDENSED MILK

1/4 **TEASPOON** VANILLA EXTRACT

PINCH OF SALT

4 **OUNCES** BITTERSWEET CHOCOLATE, FINELY CHOPPED

12 WHOLE ALMONDS

Fig & Walnut Bonbons

These are wonderful during the holidays, when you're looking for new ways to indulge in dried fruits and nuts. Arranged in little paper cups in a pretty box, they make a wonderful gift. A couple of fennel seeds hidden inside each fig give these simple candies a subtle licorice flavor. For the best result, be sure to choose plump figs rather than leathery, overly dried ones.

1. Line a large baking sheet with parchment or waxed paper.
2. Put the chocolate in a small microwave-safe bowl and microwave on high until melted, 30 seconds to 1 minute, depending on the power and size of your microwave. Stir until smooth.
3. Hold a fig half by its stem and dip it into the melted chocolate, letting the excess drip back into the bowl. Set the fig, cut side up, on the parchment. Place two fennel seeds on top of the fig, then a walnut half. Repeat with the remaining fig halves.
4. Put the baking sheet in the refrigerator and chill until the chocolate is firm, about 10 minutes. Serve immediately or keep refrigerated for up to 1 day before serving.

Makes 16

4 OUNCES BITTERSWEET CHOCOLATE, FINELY CHOPPED

8 DRIED CALMYRNA FIGS, CUT IN HALF FROM END TO END

32 FENNEL SEEDS

16 WALNUT PIECES

Caramel Chews

Chopped smokehouse almonds balance the sweetness of these quick caramel candies, making them surprisingly complex.

1. Cover a baking sheet with parchment or waxed paper.
2. Put the chocolate in a small microwave-safe bowl and microwave on high until melted, 30 seconds to 1 minute, depending on the power and size of your microwave. Stir until smooth.
3. Put a caramel in the chocolate and use a fork to turn it until it's coated on all sides. Lift it from the bowl, allowing excess chocolate to drip back into the bowl, and set it on the parchment. Sprinkle with the chopped almonds. Repeat with the remaining caramels, rewarming the chocolate in the microwave if it becomes too thick.
4. Put the baking sheet in the refrigerator until the chocolate is firm, about 10 minutes. Serve immediately or keep in an airtight container for up to 2 days before serving.

Makes 30

4 OUNCES BITTERSWEET CHOCOLATE, FINELY CHOPPED

30 KRAFT CARAMELS

¼ CUP SMOKED ALMONDS, FINELY CHOPPED

Peanut & Raisin Bark

Freezing the pan while you melt the chocolate will help the bark set up quickly.
This recipe is especially good with plump organic raisins. I love to melt chocolate with different
ingredients to make all kinds of bark. Some of my favorites are: dark chocolate, crystallized
ginger, and chopped blanched almonds. Or dark chocolate, pumpkin seeds, and crushed Heath
Bar® bits. Better yet, milk chocolate, chopped skinned hazelnuts, and a little grated orange zest; or
white chocolate, macadamia nuts, and toasted unsweetened flaked coconut.

1. Line an 8-inch-square baking pan with heavy-duty aluminum foil. Put it in the freezer while you prepare the bark.

2. In a medium-size saucepan, bring 2 inches of water to a bare simmer. Put the chocolate in a stainless-steel bowl big enough to rest on top of the saucepan and set it over the pan, making sure it doesn't touch the water. Heat, whisking a few times, until the chocolate is completely melted. Scrape the chocolate into the prepared pan and smooth into a thin layer with a small metal spatula.

3. Sprinkle the peanuts and raisins on top of the chocolate and put the pan back in the freezer for 10 minutes.

4. Lift the bark from the pan, pulling up on the foil, place it on a cutting board, and cut the bark into pieces before serving. The bark will keep in an airtight container for up to 1 week.

Makes about 12 ounces

6 OUNCES MILK CHOCOLATE, CHOPPED

1/3 CUP DRY-ROASTED PEANUTS, CHOPPED

1/3 CUP DARK RAISINS

Milk Chocolate Peanut & Raisin Bark and White Chocolate Pistachio Bark

Pistachio & Cherry Bark

The pretty colors of this simple bark make it a good choice for holiday gift-giving.
Substitute dried cranberries if you prefer their tart flavor to sweeter dried cherries.
For the shiniest bark, melt the white chocolate over very low heat until just liquid.
Higher temperatures will cause it to separate and become grainy.

1. Line an 8-inch-square baking pan with heavy-duty aluminum foil. Put it in the freezer while you prepare the bark.

2. In a medium-size saucepan, bring 2 inches of water to a bare simmer. Put the chocolate in a stainless-steel bowl big enough to rest on top of the saucepan and set it over the pan, making sure it doesn't touch the water. Heat, whisking a few times, until the chocolate is completely melted. Scrape the chocolate into the prepared pan and smooth into a thin layer with a metal spatula.

3. Sprinkle the pistachios and cherries on top of the chocolate and put the pan back in the freezer for 10 minutes.

4. Lift the bark from the pan, pulling up on the foil, place it on a cutting board, and cut the bark into pieces before serving. The bark will keep in an airtight container for up to 1 week.

Makes about 12 ounces

8 OUNCES WHITE CHOCOLATE, FINELY CHOPPED

⅓ CUP SHELLED PISTACHIOS, CHOPPED

⅓ CUP DRIED CHERRIES

Maple-Walnut Candy

Ten minutes may seem like a long time to cook the maple syrup, but it's necessary to get the candy to the right chewy, but not runny, consistency.

1. Line a rimmed baking sheet with parchment or waxed paper.
2. Combine the butter, maple syrup, and salt in a small, heavy saucepan and bring to a boil. Turn the heat to medium low and cook at a lively simmer without stirring for 10 minutes. Watch the maple syrup carefully: If it begins to burn around the edges, reduce the heat and gently tilt the pan to even out the cooking.
3. Remove the pan from the heat and stir in the walnuts. Turn the mixture out onto the prepared baking sheet and spread, using a rubber spatula, into an even layer. Let stand for 5 minutes, then put the baking sheet in the freezer for 10 minutes. Use a sharp chef's knife to cut the candy into pieces and refrigerate in an airtight container for up to 1 week until ready to serve.

Makes 2 cups

3 TABLESPOONS UNSALTED BUTTER

3/4 CUP PURE MAPLE SYRUP

1/4 TEASPOON SALT

2 CUPS WALNUT PIECES

Caramel Apples

Here's a Halloween treat that will please people who love apples as well as those who love candy. Use the smallest apples you can find. Lady apples are great, but small (no bigger than a tangerine). McIntosh, Empire, and Granny Smith apples will also work. Coat the caramel with whatever candy you like. I like the candies listed here for the way they taste or look: Toffee bars are universally appealing; Reese's Pieces® come in seasonal fall colors of orange, yellow, and brown; the cinnamon flavor of Red Hots® complements the apples; and candy corn just says Halloween.

1. Line a baking sheet with parchment or waxed paper. Place the candies in separate small bowls. Insert a craft stick into the stem end of each apple.
2. Put the unwrapped caramels and heavy cream in a medium-size, heavy saucepan over medium-low heat and stir until the caramels are melted and the mixture is smooth.
3. Hold an apple by its stick over the pot of caramel and spoon the caramel over the apple to coat, allowing the excess to drip back into the pot (if the caramel gets too stiff to spoon, reheat for a minute or two to loosen). Press the candy into the apple and place, stick side up, on the prepared baking sheet. Repeat with the remaining apples, coating two apples in each type of candy. Let stand until the caramel has cooled, about 10 minutes. The apples will keep, loosely covered with plastic wrap, at room temperature for up to 2 days.

Makes 8

ONE 1.4-OUNCE CHOCOLATE-AND-TOFFEE BAR SUCH AS SKOR®, CRUSHED

ONE 1.5-OUNCE BAG REESE'S PIECES

¼ CUP CANDY CORN

¼ CUP RED HOTS

8 SMALL APPLES, WASHED AND DRIED

ONE 14-OUNCE BAG KRAFT CARAMELS

¼ CUP HEAVY CREAM

Truffles

These truffles get their exotic flavor from green tea. I like white chocolate here; dark can be too bitter in combination with the tea. The technique is simple. Steep the tea bag in hot heavy cream, then use the infused cream to melt the chocolate. Submerge the ganache in an ice bath to cool it quickly and you are ready to roll. To make truffles quickly, limit yourself to a small batch. Big batches of melted chocolate take forever to cool down, but a mere 6 ounces will solidify in minutes.

1. Fill a large bowl with ice and water. Put the heavy cream, butter, and tea bag in a small, heavy saucepan and bring to a boil. Remove from the heat and let steep for 5 minutes.

2. Put the chocolate in a medium microwave-safe bowl and microwave on high until just melted, 1½ to 2 minutes, depending on the power and size of your microwave. Whisk until smooth.

3. Remove the tea bag from the cream mixture, squeezing it over the bowl to remove any liquid, and discard. Add to the chocolate and whisk until smooth. Set the bowl on top of the ice-filled bowl. Let cool until firm, about 20 minutes, stirring a few times.

4. Put the cocoa in a small bowl. One at a time, measure out the truffle mixture in rounded teaspoonfuls. With your palms, quickly roll each into a ball, place in the cocoa, and turn to coat. Transfer them in an airtight plastic container and freeze for 5 minutes. The truffles will keep in the refrigerator for up to 3 days until ready to serve.

Makes about 16

3 TABLESPOONS HEAVY CREAM

2 TABLESPOONS UNSALTED BUTTER, CUT INTO PIECES

1 GREEN TEA BAG

6 OUNCES WHITE CHOCOLATE, BROKEN INTO PIECES

2 TABLESPOONS UNSWEETENED COCOA POWDER

Greek Honey & Sesame Candy

Sesame seeds, so packed with exotic flavor, combine with honey to make a deliciously simple candy. If you have one, use a nonstick silicone spatula to spread the hot candy across the bottom of the pan when it is finished cooking. Otherwise, grease your spatula with nonstick cooking spray so you can work with the sticky mixture. Dipping the bottom of the pan into an ice bath will cool down the candy quickly so you can eat it in minutes. But if you aren't in a hurry, you can skip that step and let it sit at room temperature until cooled, about an hour.

1. Line an 8-inch-square baking pan with heavy-duty aluminum foil and coat with nonstick cooking spray. Fill a larger pan with ice and a little water.
2. Put the honey, sesame seeds, and salt in a small, heavy saucepan and bring to a boil. Cook over medium-high heat, stirring constantly, until the honey is golden brown, about 3 minutes.
3. Pour the mixture into the prepared baking pan. Set the pan on top of the ice-filled pan and let cool completely, about 15 minutes.
4. Turn the hardened candy out of the pan, peel away the foil, and cut into diamond shapes with a sharp chef's knife. These candies will keep in an airtight container at room temperature for 2 weeks.

Makes about ½ pound

NONSTICK COOKING SPRAY

I CUP HONEY

I CUP SESAME SEEDS

½ TEASPOON SALT

Microwave Cashew Brittle

Conventional nut brittle is a real hassle to make on top of the stove, requiring a candy thermometer and an experienced eye to judge the progress of the cooking sugar. Using the microwave simplifies the process considerably. Depending on how powerful your microwave is, your brittle mixture might need more or less time to cook. To hasten cooling, set the baking sheet on a wire rack so cool air can circulate underneath the pan. You can substitute whatever salted nuts you have on hand for the cashews—mixed nuts are delicious and give the brittle a beautiful, variegated texture.

1. Liberally grease a rimmed baking sheet with butter.
2. Combine the cashews, sugar, and corn syrup in a large microwave-safe bowl. Microwave uncovered on high for 2 minutes, then stir with a wooden spoon. Return to the microwave and cook on high until the mixture bubbles up, 1 to 3 minutes more. Stir in the butter, return to the microwave, and cook on high until the sugar turns light golden, another 3 to 5 minutes.
3. Quickly stir in the vanilla and baking soda (the mixture will bubble up) and pour onto the prepared baking sheet. Tilt the sheet back and forth to stretch the mixture into as thin a layer as possible. Let stand on a wire rack until hardened, 10 to 15 minutes, then break into pieces and store in an airtight container, the layers of brittle separated by waxed paper, for up to 1 week.

Makes about 1 pound

BUTTER FOR GREASING THE BAKING SHEET

1½ CUPS SALTED DRY-ROASTED CASHEWS

1 CUP GRANULATED SUGAR

½ CUP LIGHT CORN SYRUP

1 TABLESPOON UNSALTED BUTTER

1 TEASPOON VANILLA EXTRACT

1¼ TEASPOONS BAKING SODA

MICROWAVE CASHEW BRITTLE AND GREEK HONEY & SESAME CANDY

Caramel Popcorn & Pecans

This Cracker Jack®–like snack comes together quickly and can be endlessly varied according to taste. Try substituting pumpkin seeds or dry-roasted peanuts for the pecans, or using ⅛ teaspoon of cayenne pepper instead of the ginger.

1. Line a rimmed baking sheet with parchment or waxed paper.
2. Heat the oil in a large pot over high heat and add the popcorn. Cover and pop the corn, shaking the pan, until all of the corn is popped. Transfer the popcorn to a large bowl, add the pecans, and set aside.
3. Combine the water, sugar, and corn syrup in a large saucepan. Bring to a boil over medium-high heat. Reduce the heat to medium and cook, without stirring, until the mixture turns a light amber color, 4 to 6 minutes longer. If parts of the syrup are turning darker than others, gently tilt the pot to even out the cooking.
4. Remove the pot from the heat and stir in the butter, ginger, cinnamon, vanilla, and salt. Stir the caramel into the popcorn and pecans until the popcorn and nuts are completely coated with the caramel. Scrape out onto the prepared baking sheet and let cool, about 15 minutes, before breaking into pieces and serving. This will keep for up to 2 days in an airtight container.

Makes about 7 cups

½ TEASPOON VEGETABLE OIL

¼ CUP POPCORN KERNELS

I CUP PECAN HALVES

¼ CUP WATER

I ½ CUPS GRANULATED SUGAR

2 TABLESPOONS LIGHT CORN SYRUP

2 TABLESPOONS UNSALTED BUTTER, CUT INTO BITS

I TEASPOON GROUND GINGER

½ TEASPOON GROUND CINNAMON

I TEASPOON VANILLA EXTRACT

I ½ TEASPOONS KOSHER SALT

Liquid Dry Measures

U.S.	METRIC
¼ TEASPOON	1.25 MILLILITERS
½ TEASPOON	2.5 MILLILITERS
1 TEASPOON	5 MILLILITERS
1 TABLESPOON (3 TEASPOONS)	15 MILLILITERS
1 FLUID OUNCE (2 TABLESPOONS)	30 MILLILITERS
¼ CUP	60 MILLILITERS
⅓ CUP	80 MILLILITERS
½ CUP	120 MILLILITERS
1 CUP	240 MILLILITERS
1 PINT (2 CUPS)	480 MILLILITERS
1 QUART (4 CUPS; 32 OUNCES)	960 MILLILITERS
1 GALLON (4 QUARTS)	3.84 LITERS
1 OUNCE (BY WEIGHT)	28 GRAMS
1 POUND	454 GRAMS
2.2 POUNDS	1 KILOGRAM

Oven Temperatures

°F	GAS MARK	°C
250	½	120
275	1	140
300	2	150
325	3	165
350	4	180
375	5	190
400	6	200
425	7	220
450	8	230
475	9	240
500	10	260
550	BROIL	290

Index